BASIC CHRISTIANITY

BASIC
CHRISTIANITY

by

J. R. W. STOTT

LONDON
INTER-VARSITY FELLOWSHIP
39 BEDFORD SQUARE, W.C.1

© The Inter-Varsity Fellowship

First Edition	.	.	*March* 1958
Reprinted	.	.	*October* 1958
Reprinted	.	.	*March* 1959
Reprinted	.	.	*June* 1959
Reprinted	.	.	*March* 1960
Reprinted	.	.	*February* 1961
Reprinted	.	.	*September* 1961
Reprinted	.	.	*January* 1963
Reprinted	.	.	*May* 1964
Reprinted	.	.	*April* 1965
Reprinted	.	.	*February* 1967
Reprinted	.	.	*March* 1968

STANDARD BOOK NUMBERS:
85110 301 4 (*IVF edition*)
85110 801 6 (*International Christian Handbooks*)

Made and printed in England by
STAPLES PRINTERS LIMITED
at their Rochester, Kent, establishment

CONTENTS

ACKNOWLEDGEMENT

Unless otherwise stated the Scripture quotations in this book are from the Revised Standard Version of the Bible (copyrighted 1946 and 1952 by the Division of Christian Education, National Council of Churches, U.S.A.) and are used by permission.

PREFACE

MANY people today are friendly towards Christianity, but are not convinced of its truth. They have a sneaking suspicion that it is not intellectually respectable. They were perhaps brought up to accept it uncritically, but, when they began to ask questions for themselves, they found it easier to discard the religion of their childhood than take the trouble to investigate its credentials.

This book is written for such people. It has in view those who are thoughtfully enquiring into the truth and application of Christianity. No attempt has been made to give a comprehensive introduction either to the Christian faith or to the Christian life. I have simply tried to make a frank statement of basic Christianity.

Our starting point is the historical figure of Jesus. He was a man. He was born, He grew, He worked, He suffered and died like other men. But was He also God? Is not the deity of Jesus a rather picturesque Christian superstition? Is there any evidence for the amazing Christian assertion that the carpenter of Nazareth was the unique Son of God?

This question is fundamental. We cannot by-pass it. We must be honest. If Jesus was not God in human flesh, Christianity is exploded. We are left with just another religion with some beautiful ideas and noble ethics; its unique distinction has gone.

But there *is* evidence for the deity of Jesus—good, strong, historical, cumulative evidence; evidence to which an honest man can subscribe without committing intellectual suicide. There are Christ's extravagant claims about Himself, so bold and yet so unassuming. Then there is His incomparable character. He behaved like a visitor from another world. His strength and gentleness, His uncompromising righteousness and tender compassion, His care for children and His love for outcasts, His self-mastery and self-sacrifice, have won the admiration of the world. Moreover, His cruel death was not the end of Him. It is claimed that He rose again, and the circumstantial evidence for His resurrection is most compelling.

Supposing He was the Son of God, is basic Christianity merely an acquiescence in this truth? No. Once persuaded of the deity of Christ's person, we must examine the nature of His work. For what purpose did He visit this world? The biblical answer is, He 'came into the world to save sinners'. Jesus of Nazareth is the heaven-sent Saviour whom we sinners need. We need to be forgiven and to be restored to fellowship with the all-holy God, from whom our sins have separated us. We need to be set free from our selfishness and given strength to live up to our ideals. We need to learn to love one another, friend and foe alike. This is the meaning of 'salvation'. This is what Christ came to win for us by His death and resurrection.

Then is basic Christianity the belief that Jesus is the Son of God who came to be the Saviour of the world? No, it is not even that. To assent to Christ's divine person, to acknowledge man's need of salvation, and to believe in Christ's saving work are not enough. Christianity is not just a creed; it involves action. Our intellectual belief may be beyond criticism; but we must translate our beliefs into deeds.

What must we do, then? We must commit ourselves, heart and mind, soul and will, home and life, personally and unreservedly to Jesus Christ. We must humble ourselves before Him. We must trust in Him as *our* Saviour and submit to Him as *our* Lord; and then go on to take our place as faithful members of the Church and responsible citizens in the community.

Such is basic Christianity, and the theme of this book. But before we come to the evidence for Jesus Christ's deity, an introductory chapter on the right approach is necessary. The Christian claim is that we can find God in Jesus Christ. It should be a help to us in examining this claim if we realize both that God is Himself seeking us and that we must ourselves seek God.

J. R. W. S.

CHAPTER I

THE RIGHT APPROACH

'I N the beginning God.' These are the familiar, first four words of the Bible. They are more than an introduction to the creation story or to the Book of Genesis. They supply the key which opens our understanding to the Bible as a whole. They tell us that the religion of the Bible is a religion of the initiative of God. You can never take God by surprise. You can never anticipate Him. He always makes the first move. He is always there 'in the beginning'. Before man existed, God acted. Before man stirs himself to seek God, God has sought man. In the Bible we do not see man groping after God; we see God reaching after man. Many people visualize a god who sits comfortably on a distant throne, remote, aloof, uninterested, and indifferent to the needs of mortals, until, it may be, their importunate cries badger him into taking action on their behalf. Such a view is false to the point of blasphemy. The Bible reveals a God, who, long before it even occurs to man to turn to Him, while man is still shrouded in darkness and sunk in sin, takes the initiative, rises from His throne, lays aside His glory, and stoops to seek until He finds him.

This sovereign, anticipating activity of God is seen in many ways. He has taken the initiative in creation, bringing the universe and its contents into existence. 'In the beginning God created the heavens and the earth' (Gn. i. 1). He has taken the initiative in revelation, making known to mankind both His nature and His will. 'God, who at sundry times and in divers manners spake in time past unto the fathers by the prophets, hath in these last days spoken unto us by his Son' (Heb. i. 1, 2 AV). He has taken the initiative in salvation, coming in Jesus Christ to set men and women free from their sins. 'God . . . has visited and redeemed his people'

(Lk. i. 68). God has created. God has spoken. God has acted. These statements of God's initiative in three different spheres form a summary of the religion of the Bible. It is with the second and third that we shall be concerned in this book, because it is they which are more closely associated with Christ and Christianity. If God has spoken, His last and greatest word to the world is Jesus Christ. If God has acted, His noblest act is the redemption of the world through Jesus Christ.

God has spoken and acted in Jesus Christ. He has said something. He has done something. This means that Christianity is not just pious talk. It is not a collection of religious ideas. It is not a catalogue of rules or a string of moral exhortations. It is a 'gospel', or good news. As St. Paul wrote, it is God's good news 'concerning his Son . . . Jesus Christ' (Rom. i. 1-4). It is not primarily an invitation to man to do anything; it is supremely a declaration of what God has done in Christ for human beings like ourselves.

GOD HAS SPOKEN

Man is an insatiably inquisitive creature. His mind is so made that it cannot rest. It is always prying into the unknown. He pursues knowledge with restless energy. His life is a voyage of discovery. He is always questing, exploring, investigating, researching. He never grows out of the child's interminable 'Why?'.

Now when man's mind begins to concern itself with God, it is baffled. It gropes in the dark. It flounders out of its depth. It is lost. That this is so is not surprising because God, whatever or whoever He may be, is an immortal and infinite Being, while we are mortal and finite creatures. He is altogether beyond us. Therefore our minds, wonderfully effective instruments as they are in other realms, cannot immediately help us here. They cannot climb up into the infinite mind of God. There is no ladder. There is only a vast, unmeasured gulf. 'Can you find out the deep things of God?' (Jb. xi. 7). It is impossible. Indeed, the situation would have remained thus, if God had not taken the initiative to remedy it. Man would have remained for ever helplessly agnostic, asking indeed with Pontius Pilate, 'What is truth?' (Jn. xviii. 38), but never staying for an answer, because never daring to hope that he would receive one. He would be a worshipper, for such is his nature; but all his altars would be inscribed, 'To an unknown god' (Acts xvii. 23).

But God has spoken. He has taken the initiative to reveal Himself. The Christian doctrine of revelation is now seen to be essentially reasonable. God has 'unveiled' to our minds what would otherwise have been hidden from them. Part of His revelation is in nature. 'The heavens are telling the glory of God; and the firmament proclaims his handiwork' (Ps. xix. 1). ' . . . What can be known about God is plain to them (that is, men), because God has shown it to them. Ever since the creation of the world his invisible nature, namely, his eternal power and deity, has been clearly perceived in the things that have been made' (Rom. i. 19, 20). This is commonly called God's 'general' or 'natural' revelation.

But this is not enough. It certainly makes known to all men everywhere His existence, and something of His divine power, glory and faithfulness. But if man is to come to know God personally, to have his sins forgiven and to enter into relationship with God, he needs a more intimate and practical revelation still. The self-disclosure of God which he needs must include His holiness, His love, and His power to save from sin. This too God has been pleased to give. It is a 'special' or 'supernatural' revelation through a succession of prophets in the Old Testament and apostles in the New, but finding its chief expression in the person and work of His own Son, Jesus Christ.

The way in which the Bible explains and describes this revelation is to say that God has 'spoken'. We come to know what is in somebody else's mind most easily when he speaks. What is true of men's desire to communicate with one another is even more true of God who has desired to reveal His infinite mind to our finite minds. Since His thoughts are as much higher than our thoughts as the heavens are higher than the earth (Is. lv. 9), we could never have come to know them unless He had clothed them in words. So 'the word of the

Lord came' to many prophets, until at last Jesus Christ
came, and 'the Word became flesh and dwelt among us'
(Jn. i. 1, 14). Similarly, St. Paul writes to the Corinthian
Church (1 Cor. i. 21) ' . . . since, in the wisdom of God,
the world did not know God through wisdom, it pleased
God through the folly of what we preach to save those
who believe'. Man comes to know God not through his
own wisdom but through God's word ('what we preach'),
not through human reason but through divine revelation.
It is because God has made Himself known in Christ
that the Christian can boldly go to the agnostic and the
superstitious and say to them, as St. Paul did to the
Athenians on the Areopagus, 'What therefore you
worship as unknown, this I proclaim to you' (Acts
xvii. 23).

Much of the controversy between science and religion
has arisen through a failure to appreciate this point. The
scientific method is largely inappropriate in the sphere
of religion. Scientific knowledge advances through
observation and experiment. It works on data supplied
by the five physical senses. But when the metaphysical
is approached, there are no data. God today is neither
tangible, visible nor audible. Yet there was a time when
He chose to speak, and to clothe Himself with a body
which could be seen and touched. So St. John began his
first Epistle with the claim, 'That which was from the
beginning, which we have heard, which we have seen
with our eyes, which we have looked upon and touched
with our hands . . . we proclaim also to you . . . '
(1 Jn. i. 1-3).

GOD HAS ACTED

The Christian good news is not confined to a declaration
that God has spoken. It also affirms that God has acted.
That God has taken the initiative in both these ways is
due to the character of man's need. We are not only
ignorant; we are sinful. It is not sufficient therefore that
God should have revealed Himself to us, to dispel our
ignorance. He must also take action to save us from our
sins. So He began in Old Testament days to redeem a
people for Himself. He called Abraham from Ur, making

of him and his descendants a nation, delivering them
from slavery in Egypt, entering into a covenant with
them at Mount Sinai, leading them across the desert
into the promised land, guiding and teaching them as
His people. But all this was a preparation for His greater
deed of redemption in Christ. Men needed to be
delivered not from slavery in Egypt or from exile in
Babylon, but from their sins. It was for this principally
that Christ came. He came as a Saviour. ' . . . You shall
call his name Jesus, for he will save his people from
their sins' (Mt. i. 21). 'The saying is sure and worthy of
full acceptance, that Christ Jesus came into the world
to save sinners' (1 Tim. i. 15). He was the Son of man
who 'came to seek and to save the lost' (Lk. xix. 10). He
was like the shepherd who missed the only sheep which
was lost from the flock and went out to search until he
found it (Lk. xv. 3-7). Christianity is a religion of
salvation, and there is nothing in the other religions of
the world to compare with this message of a God who
loved, and came after, and died for, a world of lost
sinners.

MAN'S RESPONSE

God has spoken. God has acted. The record and
interpretation of these divine words and deeds is to be
found in the Bible. And there they will remain unless
we play our part. What God has said and done belongs
to history, but it must pass from past history into our
present experience. It must come out of the Bible into
our lives. God has spoken; but have we listened to His
word? God has acted; but are we benefiting from His
deed? Exactly what we must do will be unfolded in the
rest of this book. At this stage it is necessary to make
only one point, and that is, we must seek. God has
sought us. God is still seeking us. We must seek God.
God's chief quarrel with man is that he does not seek.
'The Lord looks down from heaven upon the children of
men, to see if there are any that act wisely, that seek
after God. They have all gone astray, they are all alike
corrupt; there is none that does good, no, not one' (Ps.
xiv. 2, 3). One of the most moving promises which Jesus

made was ' . . . seek and you will find . . . ' (Mt. vii. 7).
If we do not seek, we shall never find. The shepherd
searched until he found the lost sheep. The woman
searched until she found her lost coin. God is prepared
to go on seeking until He finds us. Why should we expect
to do less? God does not cast His pearls before swine.
We must seek them. God is not an ogre, playing hide-
and-seek with us in the trackless jungle of the heart and
mind, but He requires us to seek Him. He desires to be
found, but only by those who seek Him.

We must seek *diligently*. God is not honoured by a
desultory, half-hearted search. We must give our minds
to the work. 'Man is as lazy as he dares to be,' wrote
Emerson. But this matter is so serious that we must
overcome our natural sloth and apply ourselves earnestly
to the task. We seek riches and fame with great industry.
We are willing to make sacrifices for the sake of
promotion. We must with the same energy seek the
wisdom which is to be found in God only. 'If you cry
out for insight and raise your voice for understanding,
if you seek it like silver and search for it as for hidden
treasures; then you will understand the fear of the Lord
and find the knowledge of God' (Pr. ii. 3-5). God has no
patience with triflers. He has no sympathy for idlers.
But 'he is a rewarder of them that diligently seek him'
(Heb. xi. 6 AV).

We must seek *humbly*. If sloth is a hindrance to some,
pride is an even greater and commoner hindrance to
others. We must humbly admit that our minds are finite,
that they are incapable of discovering spiritual truth by
their own effort and that they depend upon God's
revelation of Himself. I am not saying that we should
suspend rational thinking. On the contrary, we are
commanded not to be like horse and mule which have
no understanding (Ps. xxxii. 9). We must use our mind;
but we must also acknowledge its limitation. This is, no
doubt, what Jesus meant when He declared, 'I thank
thee, Father, Lord of heaven and earth, that thou hast
hidden these things from the wise and understanding
and revealed them to babes' (Mt. xi. 25). It is one of
the reasons why Jesus loved little children. They are

teachable. They are not proud, self-important and critical. We need the open, humble and receptive mind of a little child.

We must seek *honestly*. We must come to what claims to be God's self-revelation not only without pride, but without prejudice; not only with a humble mind, but with an open mind. This is hard indeed. Every student knows the dangers of approaching his subject with pre-conceived notions. Much of our thought is vitiated by our presuppositions. Many enquirers approach the Bible with their minds already made up. They are not prepared to believe that Jesus of Nazareth was the unique Son of God, that He died for their sins, and that He demands their worship and trust. Therefore their minds are impervious to the evidence. 'Convince a man against his will, he's of the same opinion still.' Besides, as the years pass, our minds find it increasingly difficult to absorb new truth. They are no longer pliable. We harden into set ways and forms. Somehow we must be ready to lay aside our prejudices and open our minds to the possibility that Christianity may be true. If we are not honest and courageous enough to do this, we shall never find. God's promise is addressed only to the earnest seeker. 'You will seek me and find me; when you seek me with all your heart' (Je. xxix. 13).

We must seek *obediently*. This is the hardest condition of all to fulfil. If our will is not surrendered, our search will not end in discovery. In seeking God we have to be prepared not only to revise our ideas but to reform our lives. This is because the Christian message has a moral challenge. If the message is true, the moral challenge has to be accepted. This is a second way in which the scientific method is unsuitable in religion. The scientific research worker has to be as disinterested as possible. He must not become emotionally involved in his work. In his case the ideal is for the subject to eliminate himself altogether in his contemplation of the object. But God is not a fit object for man's detached scrutiny. You cannot fix God at the end of a telescope or a microscope and say 'How interesting!' God is not interesting. He is profoundly unsettling. The same is true of Jesus Christ.

The historical fact of Christ has religious issues because of its moral challenge. As we study, our conscience is aroused. 'We had thought intellectually to examine Him; we find He is spiritually examining us. The rôles are reversed between us. . . . We study Aristotle and are intellectually edified thereby; we study Jesus and are, in the profoundest way, spiritually disturbed. . . . We are constrained to take up some inward moral attitude of heart and will in relation to this Jesus. . . . A man may study Jesus with intellectual impartiality, he cannot do it with moral neutrality. . . . We must declare our colours. To this has our unevasive contact with Jesus brought us. We began it in the calm of the study; we are called out to the field of moral decision.'[1]

This is what Jesus meant when, addressing some unbelieving Jews, He said, 'If any man's will is to do his (that is, God's) will, he shall know whether the teaching is from God or whether I am speaking on my own authority' (Jn. vii. 17). The promise is clear. It is that we shall know whether Christ was true or false, whether His teaching was human or divine. It is the condition which is so interesting. If we want to discover whether the teaching is true, we must be willing not just to believe it, but to obey it. We shall never know if it is true unless we are ready to obey it should it be true. We must be prepared to do God's will when He makes it known.

How few seekers of this calibre are to be found! We know that the Bible is a book with a practical rather than an academic purpose. Its aim is not simply to reveal truth but to bring men to God. Therefore we cannot study it merely for fun. God has no interest in ecclesiastical dilettantes. We need to seek, not for an amusing pastime, but because this is a serious business affecting our present way of life and our future destiny. It is our hesitation to become too morally committed which hampers our search. Because we are not prepared to obey, we say we are not able to believe. Of course there are such things as genuine intellectual problems;

[1] P. Carnegie Simpson, *The Fact of Christ*, pp. 23, 24 (James Clarke 1952 edition).

but too often our vaunted unbelief is a respectable screen for our secret disobedience. It is significant that very often in the Bible the opposite of truth is not 'error' but 'evil', since it is moral evil that most frequently keeps people from seeing the truth. Thus St. Paul writes of 'men who by their wickedness suppress the truth' (Rom. i. 18), and of others who will be condemned because they 'did not believe the truth but had pleasure in unrighteousness' (2 Thes. ii. 12). I remember a young man coming to see me when he had just left school and begun work in London. He had stopped coming to church, he said, because he could not say the Creed without being a hypocrite. He no longer believed it. When he had finished his explanations, I said to him, 'If I were to answer your problems to your complete intellectual satisfaction, would you be willing to alter your manner of life?' He smiled slightly and blushed. He had been throwing off many restraints and was having a fling. His real problem was not intellectual but moral.

This, then, is the spirit in which our search must be conducted. We must cast aside sloth and pride, prejudice and sin, and seek God in scorn of the consequences. Of all these hindrances to effective search the last two are the hardest to overcome, namely intellectual prejudice and moral rebellion. Both are expressions of fear, and fear is the greatest enemy of the truth. Fear paralyses our search. We know that to find God and to accept Jesus Christ is a very inconvenient and exacting experience. We know it will involve the rethinking of our whole outlook on life, and the readjustment of our whole manner of life. And it is a combination of intellectual and moral cowardice which makes us hesitate. We do not find, because we do not seek. We do not seek because we do not want to find, and we know that the way to be certain of not finding is not to seek.

May God give you courage to seek! You may at present be wrong. Christ may be true. I urge you to become an earnest enquirer into the truth, a diligent, humble, honest, obedient seeker after God Himself. Come

to the Book which claims to be a revelation of God.
Come particularly to the Gospels which tell the story of
Jesus Christ. Give Him a chance to confront you with
Himself and to authenticate Himself to you. Come with
a gay and glad abandon of yourself to the adventure.
Come with the full consent of your mind and will, ready
to believe and obey if God convinces you. It is much
better to read the Gospels on your knees as a seeker,
than to read this book. Why not set yourself the task of
reading St. John's Gospel slowly, a chapter a day? And
before you read, pray. It does not matter how contingent
your prayer is. Perhaps you could say something like
this:

*'O God, if You exist (and I am not sure if You do),
and if You can hear this prayer (and I do not know if
You can), I want You to know that I am an honest
seeker after the truth. My mind is open; I am willing
to believe. My will is surrendered; I am ready to obey.
Teach me the truth. Show me if Jesus is Your Son and
the Saviour of the world. And if You bring conviction
to my mind, I promise that I will accept Him as my
Saviour and follow Him as my Lord. Amen.'*

No man can pray such a prayer and be disappointed.
God is no man's debtor. He honours all earnest search.
He rewards all honest seekers. He has pledged His word
to us : 'Seek, and you will find.'

I. CHRIST'S PERSON

CHAPTER II

THE CLAIMS OF CHRIST

WE have seen that it is necessary to seek if we are ever to find. But where shall we begin our search? The Christian will answer that the only place at which to begin is a person, namely the historic person of Jesus of Nazareth; for if God has spoken and acted, it is fully and finally in Jesus Christ that He has done so. The crucial issue is this: was the carpenter of Nazareth the Son of God? The great question in Christianity remains: what do you think of Christ?

This was the first question posed by the teaching and activity of Jesus during His ministry. He said to a helpless paralytic, 'Man, your sins are forgiven you', and the scribes and Pharisees began to ask, '*Who is this* that speaks blasphemies?' (Lk. v. 20, 21). It is said that He stilled a tempest on the sea of Galilee and drew from His astonished disciples the question: '*Who then is this,* that even wind and sea obey him?' (Mk. iv. 41). Those who sat at table with Him one day were amazed to hear Him grant pardon to a prostitute, and said, '*Who is this,* who even forgives sins?' (Lk. vii. 49). When Herod, the tetrarch of Galilee, heard details of the ministry of Jesus, he was perplexed. 'John I beheaded; but *who is this* about whom I hear such things?' (Lk. ix. 9). And when Jesus rode into His capital city on the back of a docile donkey, the first evangelist states that 'all the city was stirred, saying, "*Who is this?*" ' (Mt. xxi. 10).

The same question is being asked in many circles today. The person of Jesus has a strange fascination for the minds of thinking men. Professor T. W. Manson expressed his opinion on this subject in an article entitled 'Recent Studies of the Life of Christ' which appeared in *The Manchester Guardian* on 23 February 1955: 'One of the most striking features in the intellectual life of the last two centuries is the sustained interest in the life and teaching of Jesus and the sustained effort to discover the facts and to estimate their significance. One might well think that in a field so diligently cultivated over so long a period there would be nothing more to be done and little new to be said. The amazing thing is that this reasonable expectation is being constantly negatived by the event.'

There are two principal reasons why our enquiry into Christianity should begin with the person of Christ. The first is that essentially Christianity is Christ. The person and work of Christ are the foundation rock upon which the Christian religion is built. If He is not who He said He was, and if He did not do what He said He had come to do, the whole superstructure of Christianity crumbles in ruins to the ground. Take Christ from Christianity, and you disembowel it; there is practically nothing left. Christ is the centre of Christianity; all else is circumference. We are not concerned primarily to discuss the nature of His philosophy, the value of His system, or the quality of His ethics. Our concern is fundamentally with the character of His person. Dr. W. H. Griffith Thomas, formerly Principal of Wycliffe Hall, Oxford, began his book *Christianity is Christ* with the words, 'Christianity is the only religion in the world which rests on the Person of its Founder,' and went on to quote a saying of Thomas Carlyle, the nineteenth-century historian and philosopher, 'Had this doctrine of the divinity of Christ been lost, Christianity would have vanished like a dream.'

Secondly, if Jesus Christ can be shown to have been a uniquely divine person, many other problems begin naturally to be solved. The existence of God is proved and the character of God revealed if Jesus is divine. Again, questions touching man's duty and destiny, the life after death, the purpose and authority of the Old

Testament and the meaning of the cross begin to be answered because Jesus taught about these things, and His teaching must be authoritative if His person is divine.

Our investigation must therefore rightly begin with Jesus Christ, and to study Him we must turn to the Gospels. It is not necessary at this point to accept them as part of the inspired Scriptures; it will be enough to treat them as historical documents. We cannot here consider questions of their literary origin.[1] We shall be content to regard them simply as a substantially accurate record of the life and teaching of Jesus. Nor shall we be guilty of basing our case on a few obscure and isolated events and sayings. We shall seek to concentrate on what is general and plain.

Our purpose is to marshal evidence to prove that Jesus was the only begotten Son of God. We shall not be satisfied even with a verdict declaring His vague divinity; it is His unique deity which we mean to establish. We believe Him to possess an eternal and essential relation to God possessed by no other person. We regard Him neither as God in human disguise, nor as a man with divine qualities; we believe Him to be God made man. We are persuaded that Jesus was a historic person possessing two distinct and perfect natures, Godhead and manhood, and in this to be absolutely and for ever unique. Only so could He be worthy not just of our admiration but of our worship.

The evidence is threefold. It concerns the claims Christ made, His moral character and His resurrection from the dead. This chapter and the next two are devoted to a consideration of these themes. No one argument is conclusive. But the three converging lines point unfalteringly to the same conclusion.

The first witness, then, is that of Christ's own claims. In the words of Archbishop William Temple, 'It is now recognized that the one Christ for whose existence there

---

[1] For a discussion of the authenticity of the New Testament, the reader is referred to F. F. Bruce, *The New Testament Documents* (Inter-Varsity Fellowship) and Frederick G. Kenyon, *The Bible and Modern Scholarship* (John Murray).

is any evidence at all is a miraculous Figure making stupendous claims.' It is true that claims do not exactly constitute evidence, but here is a phenomenon which demands an explanation of some kind. For the sake of clarity we shall distinguish between four different kinds of claim.

1. THE EGOCENTRIC CHARACTER OF CHRIST'S TEACHING

The most striking feature of the teaching of Jesus is that He was so frequently talking about Himself. It is true that He spoke much about the Fatherhood of God, but would add that He was the Father's 'Son' who stood in a special relation to Him shared by no other person. It is also true that He went about preaching 'the good news of the kingdom of God' (Lk. iv. 43), but He regarded Himself as occupying a unique position in the kingdom. His coming inaugurated it. His mighty works extended it. Entry into it depended on men's response to Him. To 'inherit eternal life', to 'be saved', to 'enter the kingdom of God' were blessings granted only to His disciples. We are not surprised therefore to read sometimes that God's kingdom was Christ's kingdom, and that He called Himself the King (e.g. Mt. xiii. 41, xvi. 28, xx. 21, xxv. 31, 34-40; Lk. xxiii. 42; cf. Jn. xviii. 33-38). To quote from H. P. Liddon, a former Canon and Chancellor of St. Paul's Cathedral, 'His most startling revelation was Himself.'[1] This immediately sets Him apart from the other great religious teachers of the world. They are self-effacing; He is self-advancing. They point away from themselves and say, 'That is the truth, so far as I perceive it; follow that.' Jesus says, 'I am the truth; follow Me.' The founder of none of the ethnic religions has dared to say such a thing. The personal pronoun forces itself repeatedly on our attention as we read His words. For example, 'I am the bread of life; he who comes to me shall not hunger, and he who believes in me shall never thirst' (Jn. vi. 35). 'I am the

[1] H. P. Liddon, *The Divinity of our Lord and Saviour Jesus Christ* (Rivington).

light of the world; he who follows me will not walk in
darkness, but will have the light of life' (Jn. viii. 12).
'I am the resurrection and the life; he who believes in
me, though he die, yet shall he live, and whoever lives
and believes in me shall never die' (Jn. xi. 25, 26). 'I am
the way, and the truth, and the life; no one comes to the
Father, but by me' (Jn. xiv. 6).

The great question to which the first part of His
teaching led was, 'Who do you say that I am?' (Mk. viii.
29). He affirmed that Abraham had rejoiced to see His
day (Jn. viii. 56), that Moses had written of Him (Jn.
v. 46), that the Scriptures bore witness to Him (Jn. v. 39)
and that indeed in the three great divisions of the Old
Testament—the law, the prophets and the writings—
there were 'things concerning himself' (Lk. xxiv. 27, 44).
St. Luke describes in some detail the dramatic visit which
Jesus paid to the synagogue of His home village,
Nazareth. He was given a scroll of the Scriptures and He
stood up to read. The passage was Isaiah lxi. 1-2: 'The
Spirit of the Lord is upon me, because he has anointed
me to preach good news to the poor. He has sent me to
proclaim release to the captives and recovering of sight
to the blind, to set at liberty those who are oppressed, to
proclaim the acceptable year of the Lord' (Lk. iv. 18-19).
He closed the book, returned it to the synagogue
attendant and sat down, while the eyes of all the congregation were fastened on Him. He then broke the silence
with the amazing words, 'Today this scripture has been
fulfilled in your hearing.' In other words, 'Isaiah was
writing about me.'

With such an opinion of Himself, it is not surprising
that He called people to Himself. Indeed, He did not
simply issue an invitation; He uttered a command.
'Come to me', He said, and 'Follow me'. If men would
only come to Him, He promised to lift the burdens of
the weary (Mt. xi. 28-30), to satisfy the hungry (Jn. vi.
35), and to quench the thirst of the parched soul (Jn.
vi. 35 and vii. 37). Further, His followers were to obey
Him and to confess Him before men. His disciples came
to recognize the right of Jesus to make these totalitarian
claims, and in their Epistles Paul, Peter, James, and Jude

delight to call themselves His 'slaves'. More than that, He made Himself out to be the proper object both of man's faith and of his love. It is for man to believe in God, but Jesus appealed to men to believe in Himself. 'This is the work of God,' He declared, 'that you believe in him whom he has sent' (Jn. vi. 29). 'He who believes in the Son has eternal life' (Jn. iii. 36). If to believe in Him was man's first duty, not to believe in Him was his chief sin (Jn. viii. 24, xvi. 8, 9). Again, the first and great commandment is to love God with all the heart and soul and mind. Yet Jesus audaciously claimed a man's supreme love. Anyone who loved father, mother, son or daughter more than Him was not worthy of Him, He said (Mt. x. 37). Indeed, resorting to the vivid Hebrew use of contrast to convey comparison, He added: 'If any one comes to me and does not hate his own father and mother and wife and children and brothers and sisters, yes, and even his own life, he cannot be my disciple' (Lk. xiv. 26).

So convinced was He of His own central place in the purpose of God that He undertook to send Someone to take His place after He had returned to heaven. This was the Holy Spirit. Christ's favourite name for Him was the Comforter, the 'Paraclete'. It is a legal term. The word describes a barrister, an advocate, a counsel for the defence. It would be the Holy Spirit's task to plead the cause of Jesus before the world. 'He will bear witness to me', said Jesus (Jn. xv. 26). Again, 'He will glorify me, for he will take what is mine and declare it to you' (Jn. xvi. 14). The Holy Spirit's witness to the world would concern Jesus Christ. The Holy Spirit's revelation to the Church would concern Jesus Christ also. Indeed, in one more flash of breath-taking egocentricity, He predicted: 'I, when I am lifted up from the earth, will draw all men to myself' (Jn. xii. 32). He knew that the cross would exert a moral magnetism on men and women. But in drawing them, Jesus added, they would be brought primarily not to God nor to the Church, not to truth nor to righteousness, but to Himself. They would in fact be brought to these only by being brought to Him.

The most remarkable fact about this self-centred teaching is that it is uttered by One who strongly recommended humility in others. He rebuked His disciples for self-seeking and was wearied by their desire to be great. Did He not practise what He preached? He took a little child and set him in the midst as their model. Had He a different standard for Himself?

II. HIS DIRECT CLAIMS

Jesus clearly believed Himself to be the Messiah of Old Testament expectation and regarded His ministry as a fulfilment of Old Testament prediction. He had come to establish the kingdom of God foretold by generations of prophets. It is significant that the first recorded word of His public ministry was the word 'fulfilled', and His first sentence, 'The time has been fulfilled; the kingdom of God has drawn near' (Mk. i. 15, literally). He assumed the title 'Son of man' which was an accepted Messianic title derived originally from one of Daniel's visions. He accepted the description 'Son of God' when challenged by the high priest (Mk. xiv. 61, 62), which was another Messianic title taken particularly from Psalm ii. 7. He also interpreted His mission in the light of the portrayal of the suffering servant of Jehovah in the latter part of the Book of Isaiah. The first stage in His instruction of the Twelve culminated in the incident at Caesarea Philippi when Simon Peter confessed his faith in Jesus as the Christ (Mk. viii. 27-29). Others might suppose Jesus to be one of the prophets; but Simon had come to recognize Him as the One to whom the prophets pointed. He was not just another signpost, but the destination to which the signposts had led. The whole ministry of Jesus is coloured by this sense of fulfilment. 'Blessed are the eyes which see what you see!' He once said privately to His disciples. 'For I tell you that many prophets and kings desired to see what you see, and did not see it, and to hear what you hear, and did not hear it' (Lk. x. 23, 24; cf. Mt. xiii. 16, 17).

But the direct claims with which we are now

concerned refer not just to His Messiahship but to His deity. He claimed to be the Son of God not only in the messianic sense but to describe the unique and eternal relationship with God which He possessed. Three examples of this greater claim may be given.

First, there is the close association with God as His 'Father' of which He constantly spoke. Even as a boy of twelve He astonished His human parents by His uncompromising zeal for His heavenly Father's business (Lk. ii. 49). 'My Father is working still, and I am working' (Jn. v. 17). 'I and the Father are one' (Jn. x. 30). 'I am in the Father and the Father in me' (Jn. xiv. 10, 11). 'My Father will love him, and we will come to him and make our home with him' (Jn. xiv. 23). It is true that He taught His disciples to address God as 'Father' too, but so different is Christ's sonship from ours that He was obliged to distinguish between them. To Him God is 'my Father' (Mt. xviii. 10, 19, 35, vii. 21, xx. 23, xxvi. 53). He therefore said to Mary Magdalene, 'I am ascending to my Father and your Father' (Jn. xx. 17). It would not have been possible for Him to say, 'I ascend to *our* Father.' These verses are all taken from St. John's Gospel, but the same unique relationship with God is claimed by Jesus in Matthew xi. 27 where He says, 'All things have been delivered to me by my Father; and no one knows the Son except the Father, and no one knows the Father except the Son and any one to whom the Son chooses to reveal him.' That Jesus claimed this intimate relation to God is further suggested by the indignation which He aroused in the Jews 'because he has made himself the Son of God' (Jn. xix. 7). So close was His connection with God that He equated a man's attitude to Himself with his attitude to God. Thus, to know Him was to know God (Jn. viii. 19, xiv. 7); to see Him was to see God (Jn. xii. 45, xiv. 9); to believe in Him was to believe in God (Jn. xii. 44, xiv. 1); to receive Him was to receive God (Mk. ix. 37); to hate Him was to hate God (Jn. xv. 23); and to honour Him was to honour God (Jn. v. 23).

We pass now from a consideration of Christ's general claim to close personal relation to God to two examples

of his more particular and direct claims. The first
occurs at the conclusion of the eighth chapter of St.
John's Gospel. In controversy with the Jews, Jesus
asserts, 'Truly, truly, I say to you, if any one keeps my
word, he will never see death.' This is too much for His
critics. 'Abraham died,' they expostulate, 'as did the
prophets; . . . Are you greater than our father
Abraham . . . ? Who do you claim to be?' 'Your father
Abraham rejoiced that he was to see my day,' replies
Jesus. The Jews are yet more perplexed. 'You are not
yet fifty years old, and have you seen Abraham?' And
Jesus responds with one of the most pregnant claims He
ever made, 'Truly, truly, I say to you, before Abraham
was, I am' (Jn. viii. 51-58). Then they took up stones to
throw at Him. Now the law of Moses made stoning the
penalty of blasphemy, and at first sight one wonders
what they saw to be blasphemous in Christ's words. Of
course there was the claim to have lived before
Abraham. This He frequently made. He had 'come
down' from heaven and 'been sent' by the Father. But
that claim was tolerably innocent. We must look further.
We notice that He had not said 'Before Abraham was
I was', but 'I am'. It was therefore a claim to have been
existing eternally before Abraham. But even that is not
all. There is more in this 'I am' than a claim to eternity;
there is a claim to deity. 'I am' is the divine Name by
which Jehovah had revealed Himself to Moses, at the
burning bush. 'I am who I am . . . say this to the people
of Israel, "I am has sent me to you"' (Ex. iii. 14). This
divine title Jesus quietly takes to Himself. It is because
of this that the Jews reached out for stones to avenge
the blasphemy.

The second example of a direct claim to deity took
place after the resurrection (if for the moment we may
assume that the resurrection took place). The Sunday
following Easter Day, incredulous Thomas is with the
other disciples in the upper room when Jesus appears.
He invites Thomas to feel His wounds, and Thomas,
overwhelmed with wonder, cries out, 'My Lord and my
God!' (Jn. xx. 26-29). Jesus accepts the designation. He
rebukes Thomas for his unbelief, but not for his worship.

III. HIS INDIRECT CLAIMS

The claim to deity advanced by our Lord was made as forcefully by indirect as by direct means. The implications of His ministry were as eloquent a testimony to His person as His plain statements. On many occasions He exercised functions which belong properly to God. He assumed prerogatives which are essentially divine. Of these four may be mentioned. The first is the claim to forgive sins. On two separate occasions Jesus forgave sinners. The first time a paralytic was brought to Him by his friends and let down on his pallet bed through the roof. Jesus saw that his need was basically spiritual and surprised the crowd by saying to him, 'My son, your sins are forgiven' (Mk. ii. 1-12). The second declaration of forgiveness was made to a fallen woman. Jesus was taking a meal in a Pharisee's house when an unknown woman came behind Him as He reclined at table, washed His feet with her tears and wiped them with her hair, kissed them and anointed them with ointment. And Jesus said to her, 'Your sins are forgiven' (Lk. vii. 36-50). On both occasions the bystanders raised their eyebrows and asked, 'Who is this? What blasphemy is this? Who can forgive sins but God only?' Their questions were correctly worded. We may forgive the injuries which others do to us; but only God can forgive the sins we commit against Him.

Christ's second indirect claim was to bestow life. He described Himself as 'the bread of life' (Jn. vi. 35), 'the life' (Jn. xiv. 6) and 'the resurrection and the life' (Jn. xi. 25). He likened His people's dependence on Him to the sustenance derived from the vine by its branches. He offered a Samaritan woman 'living water' (Jn. iv. 10-15) and promised eternal life to the rich young ruler if he would come and follow Him (Mk. x. 17, 21). He called Himself the Good Shepherd who would not only give His life for the sheep but give life to them (Jn. x. 28). He stated that God had given Him authority over all flesh that He should give life to as many as God gave Him (Jn. xvii. 2), and declared, 'the Son gives life to whom he will' (Jn. v. 21). So definite was this claim that His disciples clearly recognized its truth. It made declension from Him impossible. 'To whom shall we go?' asked Peter. 'You have the words of eternal life' (Jn. vi. 68). Now all this is significant because life is an enigma. Whether it be physical life or spiritual, its nature is as baffling as its origin. We can neither define what it is nor state whence it comes. We can only call it a divine gift. It is this gift which Jesus claimed to bestow.

Christ's third indirect claim was to teach the truth. It is not so much the truths which He taught as the direct and dogmatic manner in which He taught them which calls for notice. His contemporaries were certainly impressed by His wisdom. 'Where did this man get all this? What is the wisdom given to him? . . . Is not this the carpenter . . . ?' (Mk. vi. 3). Again, 'How is it that this man has learning, when he has never studied?' (Jn. vii. 15). They also noticed the graciousness of His speech (Lk. iv. 22). But they were more impressed still by His authority, 'No man ever spoke like this man' (Jn. vii. 46). They were astonished at His doctrine, 'for his word was with authority' (Lk. iv. 32). Again, at the conclusion of the sermon on the mount, it is recorded, 'when Jesus finished these sayings, the crowds were astonished at his teaching, for he taught them as one who had authority, and not as their scribes' (Mt. vii. 28, 29). His was not even the authority of a prophet, for it was not derived; it was direct. His formula was not 'Thus says the Lord', but 'Truly, truly, I say to you'. It is true that He described His doctrine as being not His but the Father's who had sent Him (Jn. vii. 17, 18). Nevertheless, He knew Himself to be such an immediate organ of divine revelation as to be able to speak with great personal assurance. He never hesitated or apologized. He had no need to contradict, withdraw or modify anything He said. He spoke the unequivocal words of God (Jn. iii. 34). He predicted the future with complete conviction. He issued absolute moral commands like 'Love your enemies' (Mt. v. 44; Lk. vi. 27), 'Do not be anxious about to-morrow' (Mt. vi. 34), 'Judge not, that you be not judged' (Mt. vii. 1). He made promises of whose fulfilment He had no doubt, 'Ask, and it will be given you' (Mt. vii. 7; Lk. xi. 9). He asserted that

His words were as eternal as the law, and would never pass away (Mk. xiii. 31; cf. Mt. v. 18). He warned His hearers that their destiny depended on their response to His word, as the destiny of Israel had depended on their response to Jehovah's word (Mt. vii. 24-27; Jn. xii. 48).

Christ's fourth indirect claim was to judge the world. This is perhaps the most fantastic of all His statements. Several of His parables imply that He will come back at the end of the world. Moreover, the final day of reckoning will be postponed until His return. He will Himself arouse the dead (Jn. v. 28, 29), and all the nations will be gathered before Him. He will sit on the throne of His glory, and all judgment will be committed to Him by the Father (Jn. v. 22). He will then separate men from one another as a shepherd separates the sheep from the goats. Some will be invited to come and inherit the kingdom prepared for them from the foundation of the world. Others will hear the dreadful words, 'Depart from me, you cursed, into the eternal fire prepared for the devil and his angels' (Mt. xxv. 31-46). Not only will Jesus be the Judge, but the criterion of judgment will be men's attitude to Him as revealed in their treatment of His 'brethren', who are His followers who do the will of God (Mk. iii. 35), or in their response to His word (Jn. xii. 47, 48). Those who have acknowledged Him before men He will acknowledge before His Father: those who have denied Him, He will deny (Mt. x. 32, 33). Indeed, for a man to be excluded from heaven on the last day, it will be enough for Jesus to say, 'I never knew you' (Mt. vii. 23). It is hard to exaggerate the magnitude of this claim. Imagine a minister addressing his congregation in these terms today: 'Listen attentively to my words. Your eternal destiny depends on it. I shall return at the end of the world to judge you, and your fate will be settled according to your obedience to me.' Such a preacher would not long escape the attentions of the police or the psychiatrists.

IV. CHRIST'S DRAMATIZED CLAIMS

It only remains for us to consider the miracles of Christ,

which we may describe as His dramatized claims. This is
no place for a thorough discussion of the possibility and
purpose of miracles. It is enough to indicate that the
value of Christ's miracles lies less in their supernatural
character than in their spiritual significance. They are
'signs' as well as 'wonders'. They are never performed
selfishly or senselessly. Their purpose is not to show off
or to compel submission. They are not merely demon-
strations of physical power, but illustrations of moral
authority. They are in fact the acted parables of Jesus.
They exhibit His claims visually. They are His works
which dramatize His words. St. John saw this clearly
and constructs his Gospel round six or seven selected
'signs' (Jn. xx. 30, 31), and associates them with the great
'I am' declarations which Christ made. Thus, the first
sign was the changing of water into wine at a wedding
reception in Cana of Galilee. It is not in itself a particularly edifying miracle. Its significance lies beneath the
surface. John tells us that the waterpots of stone stood
ready 'for the Jewish rites of purification' (Jn. ii. 6).
This is the clue we are seeking. The water stood for the
old religion, like Jacob's well in chapter iv, rich in Old
Testament associations. The wine stood for the religion
of Jesus. As Christ changed the water into wine, so the
gospel would supersede the law. The sign advanced the
claim that He was competent to inaugurate the new
order. He was the Messiah. As He was soon to say to the
Samaritan woman, 'I . . . am he' (Jn. iv. 26).

Similarly, His feeding of the five thousand illustrated
His claim to satisfy the hunger of the human heart. 'I
am the bread of life,' He said (Jn. vi. 35). A little later,
He opened the eyes of a man born blind, having
previously said, 'I am the light of the world' (Jn. viii. 12).
If He could restore sight to the blind, He could open
the eyes of men to see and to know God. Finally, He
brought back to life a man called Lazarus who had been
dead four days, and claimed, 'I am the resurrection and
the life' (Jn. xi. 25). He had resuscitated a dead man. It
was a sign. The life of the body symbolized the life of the
soul. Christ could be the life of the Christian believer
before death and would be the resurrection of the

Christian believer after death. All these miracles are
parables, for men are spiritually hungry, blind and dead,
and only Christ can satisfy their hunger, restore their
sight and raise them to newness of life.

CONCLUSION

It is not possible to eliminate these claims from the
teaching of the carpenter of Nazareth. It cannot be said
that they were invented by the evangelists, nor even
that they were unconsciously exaggerated. They are
widely and evenly distributed in the different Gospels
and sources of the Gospels, and the portrait of this
Teacher is too consistent and too balanced to have been
imagined. The claims are there. They do not in themselves constitute evidence of deity. The claims may have
been false. But some explanation of them must be found.
We cannot any longer regard Jesus as simply a great
Teacher, if He was so grievously mistaken in one of the
chief subjects of His teaching, namely Himself. There
is a certain disturbing 'megalomania' about Jesus which
many scholars have recognized. 'These claims', wrote
Dr. P. T. Forsyth, 'in a mere man would be egoism
carried even to imperial megalomania.'[1] Again, 'The
discrepancy between the depth and sanity, and (let me
add) *shrewdness,* of His moral teaching and the rampant
megalomania which must lie behind His theological
teaching unless He is indeed God, has never been
satisfactorily got over'.[2]

Was He a deliberate impostor? Did He attempt to
gain the adherence of men to His views by assuming a
divine authority He did not possess? This is very difficult
to believe. There is something so guileless about Jesus.
He hated hypocrisy in others and was transparently
sincere Himself.

Was He sincerely mistaken then? We need not call
Him mad; but had He a fixed delusion about Himself?
This possibility has its protagonists, but one suspects

[1] P. T. Forsyth, *This Life and the Next.*
[2] C. S. Lewis, *Miracles,* p. 132.

that their delusion is greater than His. Jesus does not give the impression of that abnormality which one expects to find in the deluded. His character appears to support His claims, and it is in this sphere that we must now pursue our investigation.

CHAPTER III

THE CHARACTER OF CHRIST

SOME years ago I received a letter from a young man with whom I had some slight acquaintance. 'I have just made a great discovery', he wrote. 'Almighty God had two Sons. Jesus Christ was the first; I am the second.' I glanced at the address at the top of his letter. He was writing from a mental hospital.

There have of course been many pretenders to greatness and to divinity. Lunatic asylums are full of deluded wretches who claim to be Julius Caesar, the Prime Minister, the Emperor of Japan or Jesus Christ. But no one believes them. No one is deceived except themselves. They have no disciples, except perhaps their fellow patients. They fail to convince other people simply because they do not seem to be what they claim to be. Their character does not support their claims.

Now the Christian's conviction about Christ is greatly strengthened by the fact that He did appear to be what He said He was. There is no discrepancy between His words and His deeds. Certainly a very remarkable character would be necessary to authenticate His extravagant claims, but we believe that He displayed just such a character. His character does not conclusively prove His claims to be true, but it is congruous with them. His claims were exclusive. His character was unique. John Stuart Mill called Him 'A unique Figure, not more unlike all His predecessors than all His followers'.[1] 'Instinctively', wrote Carnegie Simpson, 'we do not class Him with others. When one reads His name in a list beginning with Confucius and ending with Goethe we feel it is an offence less against orthodoxy than against decency. Jesus is not one of the group of the world's great. Talk about Alexander the Great and Charles the Great and Napoleon the Great if you will. . . . Jesus is

[1] Quoted by W. H. Griffith Thomas, *Christianity is Christ*, p. 15.

apart. He is not the Great; He is the Only. He is simply Jesus. Nothing could add to that. . . . He is beyond our analyses. He confounds our canons of human nature. He compels our criticism to overleap itself. He awes our spirits. There is a saying of Charles Lamb . . . that "if Shakespeare was to come into this room we should all rise up to meet him, but if that Person was to come into it, we should all fall down and try to kiss the hem of His garment".[1]

We are concerned then to show that Jesus stands in a moral category by Himself. To concede that He was 'the greatest man who ever lived' does not begin to satisfy us. We cannot talk of Jesus in comparative, or even superlative, terms. To us it is a question not of comparison, but of contrast. 'Why do you call me good?' He asked the rich young ruler. 'No one is good but God alone.' 'Exactly', we should have replied. 'It is not that You are better than other men, nor even that You are the best of men, but that You are good—good with the absolute goodness of God.'

The importance of this claim should be clear. Sin is a congenital disease among men. We are born with its infection in our nature. It is a universal complaint. Therefore if Jesus of Nazareth was without sin, He was no mere man as we know men. If He was sinless, He was distinct from you and me. He was supernatural. 'His character was more wonderful than the greatest miracle.'[2] As Professor James Denney, of the United Free College, Glasgow, wrote in his book *Studies in Theology:* 'This separateness from sinners is not a little, but a stupendous thing; it is the presupposition of redemption; it is that very virtue in Christ without which He would not be qualified to be a Saviour, but would, like us, need to be saved.'

It may be helpful to summarize the evidence for the sinlessness of Christ under four headings.

I. WHAT CHRIST HIMSELF THOUGHT

On one or two occasions Jesus stated directly that He

[1] P. Carnegie Simpson, *The Fact of Christ*, pp. 19-22.
[2] Tennyson, quoted by Carnegie Simpson, *op. cit.*

was without sin. When a woman was discovered in the act of adultery and was dragged before Jesus, He issued an embarrassing challenge to her accusers, 'Let him who is without sin among you be the first to throw a stone at her.' Gradually they slunk away until there was no one left (Jn. viii. 1-11). A little later in the same chapter, St. John records that Jesus issued another challenge, this time concerning Himself, 'Which of you convicts me of sin?' (verse 46). No one answered. They slipped away when He accused them. But when He invited them to accuse Him, He could stay and bear their scrutiny. They were all sinners; He was without sin. He lived a life of perfect obedience to His Father's will. 'I always do', He said, 'what is pleasing to him' (verse 29). There was nothing boastful about those words. He spoke naturally, with neither fuss nor pretension.

Similarly, by the very nature of His teaching, He placed Himself in a moral category by Himself. So did the Pharisee in the Temple in his blasphemous thanksgiving, 'God, I thank thee that I am not like the rest of men' (Lk. xviii. 11, literally). But Jesus assumed His uniqueness unself-consciously. He did not need to draw attention to it. It was a fact so obvious to Him that it hardly required emphasis. It was implied rather than asserted. All other men were lost sheep; He had come as the Good Shepherd to seek and to save them. All other men were sick with the disease of sin; He was the Physician who had come to heal them. All other men were plunged in the darkness of sin and ignorance; He was the light of the world. All other men were sinners; He was born to be their Saviour and would shed His blood in death for the forgiveness of their sins. All other men were hungry; He was the bread of life. All other men were dead in trespasses and sins; He could be their life now and their resurrection hereafter. He stated these truths in the most unassuming manner, not to impress them with His greatness but to arouse their faith, so that He might meet their needs.

It is not surprising, therefore, that although we are told of the temptations of Jesus, we hear nothing of His sins. He never confesses His sins or asks for forgiveness, although He tells His disciples to do so. He manifests no consciousness of moral failure. He appears to have no feeling of guilt and no sense of estrangement from God. His baptism was indeed John's 'baptism of repentance', but John demurred before baptizing Christ, and Christ submitted to it not because He recognized Himself to be a sinner but 'to fulfil all righteousness' (Mt. iii. 15), and to begin to identify Himself with the sins of the world. He Himself seems to have lived in unbroken communion with His Father. Griffith Thomas quotes the words of the nineteenth-century German theologian, David Strauss, who wrote that He had a 'conscience unclouded by the memory of any sins'.[1]

Now this absence of all moral discontent and this sense of unclouded fellowship with God are particularly remarkable for two reasons. The first is that Jesus possessed a very keen moral judgment. To borrow an expression from the Epistle to the Hebrews, He could discern 'the thoughts and intentions of the heart' (iv. 12). 'He . . . knew what was in man' (Jn. ii. 25). Often it is recorded of Him in the Gospel narratives that He read the inner questionings and perplexities of the crowd. His clear perception led Him fearlessly to expose the duplicity of the Pharisees. He hated their hypocrisy. He pronounced woes upon them as thunderous as those of the Old Testament prophets. Ostentation and pretence were an abomination to Him. Yet His penetrating eye saw no sin in Himself. Although He abhorred self-righteousness in others, He detected none in Himself when He declared Himself to be righteous.

The second reason why His self-conscious purity is astonishing is that it is utterly unlike the experience of all saints and mystics. The Christian knows that the nearer he approaches God, the more he becomes aware of his sin. In this the saint resembles the modern scientist. The more the scientist discovers, the more he appreciates the mysteries which await his discovery. So the more the saint grows in likeness to Christ, the more he perceives the vastness of the distance which still separates him from his ideal. A glance into any Christian biography

[1] *Christianity is Christ*, p. 18.

will satisfy the reader of this fact, if his own experience is not sufficient evidence. One example may be given. David Brainerd was a young pioneer missionary among the Indians of Delaware at the beginning of the nineteenth century. His diary and letters reveal the rich quality of his devotion to Christ. Despite great pain and crippling weakness which led to his death at the early age of twenty-nine, he gave himself without reserve to his work. He travelled on horseback through thick forests, preached and taught without rest, slept in the open, and was content with no settled home or family life. His diary is full of expressions of love to 'my dear Indians' and of prayers and praises to his Saviour. Here surely, one would imagine, is a saint of the first order, whose life and work can have been little tainted by sin. Yet as we turn the pages of his diary, he again and again laments his moral 'corruption'. He complains of his lack of prayer and love for Christ. He calls himself 'a poor worm', 'a dead dog', and 'an unspeakably worthless wretch'. He was not morbid or falsely self-accusing. He simply lived near Christ and was painfully aware of his sinfulness.

'And they who fain would serve Thee best
Are conscious most of wrong within.'

Yet Christ, who lived more closely to God than any other, was free from all sense of sin.

II. WHAT CHRIST'S FRIENDS SAID

It is clear then that Christ believed Himself to be sinless, as He believed Himself to be the Messiah and the Son of God. But may He not have been mistaken in the former as in the latter? What did His disciples think? Did they share His opinion of Himself?

It may be thought that the disciples of Christ were poor witnesses. It has been argued that they were biased, and that they deliberately painted Him in more beautiful colours than He deserved. But the apostles have been greatly maligned. Their testimony is far more valuable than has often been supposed, and their statements on this subject cannot be so lightly dismissed. There are several reasons why we may confidently rely on their evidence. First, because they lived in close intimacy with Jesus for about three years. They ate and slept together. They experienced the cramped neighbourliness of the same boat. They even had a common purse (and a common bank account can be a most fruitful cause of dissension!). The disciples got on one another's nerves, and many were the quarrels which broke out among them. But they never found in Him the sins they found in themselves. Familiarity normally breeds contempt, but not in this case. Indeed, two of the chief witnesses to the sinlessness of Christ are Peter and John (as we shall see later), and they belonged to that inner group (consisting of Peter, James and John), to whom He gave special privileges and a yet more intimate revelation.

Second, the testimony of the apostles is reliable in this matter because they were Jews whose minds had been soaked since infancy in the doctrines of the Old Testament. And one Old Testament doctrine which they cannot have escaped is the universality of human sin. 'All we like sheep have gone astray' (Is. liii. 6). 'There is none that does good, no, not one' (Ps. xiv. 3). If, as must be the case, they had imbibed this teaching, they would not easily have attributed sinlessness to anyone.

Third, the apostolic testimony to the sinlessness of Jesus is the more credible because it is indirect. They do not set out to establish the truth that He was without sin. Their remarks are asides. They are discussing some other subject, and add almost as a parenthesis a reference to His sinlessness. In this at least their affirmations cannot be described as tendentious.

This is what they say. Peter first describes Jesus as 'a lamb without blemish or spot' (1 Pet. i. 19) and then goes on to say that He 'did no sin; neither was guile found in his mouth' (1 Pet. ii. 22 AV). St. John in the early part of his first Epistle roundly declares that all men are sinners, and that if we say we have no sin or have not sinned, we are both liars ourselves and make God a liar too (1 Jn. i. 8-10). But he goes on to say that in Christ, who was manifested to take away our sins, there is no sin (1 Jn. iii. 5). To this testimony of Peter and John,

we may add the words of St. Paul and of the author of
the Epistle to the Hebrews. St. Paul describes Jesus as
One who 'knew no sin' (2 Cor. v. 21), and in the Epistle
to the Hebrews He, as our 'high priest', is said to be
'holy, blameless, unstained, separated from sinners,
exalted above the heavens' (vii. 26). He was indeed
'tempted in all points as we are'—but 'without sinning'
(iv. 15).

III. WHAT CHRIST'S ENEMIES CONCEDED

When considering what the enemies of Jesus thought of
Him we may feel ourselves to be on safer ground. They
certainly had no bias—at least not in His favour. We
read in the Gospels that 'they watched him' (Mk. iii. 2).
They tried to 'entrap him in his talk' (Mk. xii. 13).
It is well known that when a debate cannot be won by
argument, controversialists are prone to descend to
personal abuse. If reasons are lacking, mud is a good
substitute. Even the annals of the Church are smudged
by the dirt of personal animosities. So it was with the
enemies of Jesus. He was more than a match for them
in discussion, so they sought for other excuses for their
venom.

We must carefully consider their criticisms. St. Mark
assembles four of their attacks in ii. 1—iii. 6. Their first
accusation was blasphemy. Jesus had forgiven a man's
sins. This was an invasion of divine territory. This was
blasphemous arrogance, they said. But to say so is to beg
the supreme question. If He were indeed divine, to
forgive sins was His prerogative. Next, they were (they
said) horrified by His evil associations. He fraternized
with sinners. He ate with publicans. He rubbed shoulders
with harlots. No Pharisee would dream of this behaviour.
He would gather his skirts around him and recoil from
contact with such scum. He would have thought himself
righteous for doing so, too. He would not appreciate the
grace and tenderness of Jesus who, though 'separate from
sinners', yet earned the honoured title 'friend of sinners'.

Their third accusation was that His religion was
frivolous. He did not fast like the Pharisees, or even like
the disciples of John the Baptist. He was a 'glutton and

a drunkard' who came 'eating and drinking' (Mt. xi. 19).
Such an attack hardly deserves a serious refutation. That
Jesus was full of joy is our boast, and there can be no
doubt that He took religion seriously.

Fourth, they were incensed by His sabbath-breaking.
He healed on the sabbath day, and His disciples even
walked through the cornfields on the sabbath, plucking,
rubbing and eating corn. To the scribes and Pharisees
this was tantamount to reaping and threshing, and was
strictly forbidden by their traditions! But no honest
student can doubt that Jesus had a high regard for the
law of God. He obeyed it Himself, and in controversy
He referred His opponents to it as the arbiter. He also
affirmed that God had made the sabbath, but that He
had made it for man's benefit. He claimed the right to
break the scribal rules and, being Himself the 'Lord of
the sabbath', to give a proper interpretation of the divine
law.

All these accusations are either trivial or question-
begging. And when the end came and Jesus was on trial
for His life, His detractors had to hire false witnesses
against Him, and even they did not agree with one
another. Moreover, the only charge they could manufacture against Him was not moral but political. And
as the stately Prisoner came before men and women for
a verdict, again and again He was pronounced righteous.
Pilate, after several cowardly attempts to evade the issue,
publicly washed his hands and declared himself 'innocent
of this man's blood' (Mt. xxvii. 24). The very phrase he
used seems reminiscent of the message his wife had sent
him after a troublesome dream had disturbed her: 'Have
nothing to do with that righteous man' (Mt. xxvii. 19).
Herod could find no fault in Him either (Lk. xxiii. 15).
Judas the traitor, filled with remorse, returned the thirty
pieces of silver to the priests with the words 'I have
sinned in betraying innocent blood' (Mt. xxvii. 3, 4). The
penitent thief on the cross rebuked his confederate for
his abuse and added, 'this man has done nothing wrong'
(Lk. xxiii. 41). Finally, the centurion, having watched
Christ suffer and die, exclaimed, 'Certainly this man was
innocent!' (Lk. xxiii. 47).

IV. OUR OWN ESTIMATE OF CHRIST

But we do not need to rely on the testimony of others, we can see for ourselves. The moral perfection of Jesus which was quietly claimed by Him, confidently asserted by His apostles and reluctantly acknowledged by His enemies, is clearly exhibited in the Gospels.

We are given ample opportunity to form our own judgment. The picture of Jesus painted by the evangelists is a comprehensive one. True, it depicts largely His public ministry of only about three years. But we are given a glimpse of His boyhood, and St. Luke twice repeats that during His hidden years at Nazareth He was developing naturally in body, mind and spirit, and was growing in favour with God and man (Lk. ii. 40, 52). We see Him withdrawn into privacy with His disciples, and we watch Him in the noisy bustle of the crowd. He is brought before us in the Galilean ministry, hero-worshipped by the mob who wanted to take Him by force and make Him a King after their own pattern, and we follow Him into Jerusalem and the cloisters of the Temple where Pharisees and Sadducees unite in their subtle inquisition. But whether scaling the dizzy heights of success or plunged into the depths of bitter rejection alone, He is the same Jesus. He is consistent. He has no moods. He does not change.

Again, the portrait is balanced. There is in Him no trace of the crank. He believes ardently in what He teaches, but He is no fanatic. His doctrine is unpopular, but He is not eccentric. There is as much evidence for His humanity as for His divinity. He gets tired. He needs to sleep and eat and drink like other men. He experiences the human emotions of love and anger, joy and sorrow. He is fully human, but He is no mere man.

Above all, He was unselfish. Nothing is more striking than this. Believing Himself to be divine, He yet did not put on airs or stand on His dignity. He was never pompous as men tend to be who think themselves greater than they are. There was no touch of self-importance about Jesus. He was humble. It is this paradox which is so baffling, the self-centredness of His teaching and the unself-centredness of His behaviour. In thought He put

Himself first; in deed last. He combined in Himself the greatest self-esteem and the greatest self-sacrifice. He knew Himself to be the Lord of all, but He became the servant of all. 'The Son of man' (He said) 'came not to be served but to serve, and to give his life as a ransom for many' (Mk. x. 45). His renunciations are tremendous. It is claimed (by Him as well as by us) that He renounced the joys of heaven for the sorrows of earth, exchanging an eternal immunity to the approach of sin for painful contact with evil in this world. He was born of a lowly Hebrew mother in a dirty stable in the small village of Bethlehem. He became a refugee baby in Egypt. He was brought up in the obscure hamlet of Nazareth, and toiled at a carpenter's bench to support His mother and the other children in their home. In due time He became an itinerant preacher. He had few possessions, small comforts and no home. He made friends with simple fishermen and publicans. He bore with His disciples' strife and folly, and washed their feet like a slave. He touched lepers and allowed harlots to touch Him. He gave Himself away in a ministry of continuous healing and helping, teaching and preaching. He was misunderstood and misrepresented, and became the victim of men's prejudices and vested interests. He was despised and rejected by His own people, and deserted by His own friends. He gave His back to be flogged, His face to be spat upon, His head to be crowned with thorns, His hands and feet to be nailed to a common Roman gallows. And as the cruel spikes were driven home, He kept praying for His tormentors, 'Father, forgive them; for they know not what they do.'

Such a man is altogether beyond our reach. He succeeded just where we invariably fail. He had complete self-mastery. He never retaliated. He never grew resentful or irritable. He had such control of Himself that, whatever men might think or say or do, He would deny Himself and abandon Himself to the will of God and the welfare of mankind. 'I seek not my own will', He said, and 'I do not seek my own glory' (Jn. v. 30, viii. 50). As St. Paul wrote, 'For Christ did not please himself' (Rom. xv. 3). This utter disregard of self in the service of God and man is what the Bible calls love. There is no self-interest in love. The essence of love is self-sacrifice. The worst of men is adorned by an occasional flash of such nobility, but the life of Jesus irradiated it with a never-fading incandescent glow. The conclusion of the matter is this: Jesus was sinless because He was selfless. Such selflessness is love. And God is love.

CHAPTER IV

THE RESURRECTION OF CHRIST

WE have considered the extravagant claims which Jesus made, and observed the selfless character which He displayed. We are now to examine the evidence for His historical resurrection from the dead.

Clearly the resurrection has great significance. If it can be shown that Jesus of Nazareth rose from the dead, it is beyond dispute that He was a unique figure. It is not a question of His spiritual survival, nor of His physical resuscitation, but of His conquest of death and His resurrection to a new plane of existence altogether. We do not know of anyone else who has had this experience. Modern man is therefore as scornful as the Athenian philosophers who heard St. Paul preach on the Areopagus: 'When they heard of the resurrection of the dead, some mocked' (Acts xvii. 32).

We may not feel that His resurrection establishes His deity conclusively, but we must agree that it is suggestive of it. It is fitting that a supernatural person should enter and leave the earth in a supernatural way. This is in fact what the New Testament teaches and the Church believes. His birth was natural, but His conception was supernatural. His death was natural, but His resurrection was supernatural. His miraculous conception and resurrection do not prove His deity, but they are congruous with it. We are not concerned here with His so-called 'Virgin Birth'.[1] There is good reason to believe it, but it is not used in the New Testament to prove Him Messiah and Son of God, as is the resurrection. Jesus Himself never predicted His passion without adding that He would rise, and described His coming resurrection as a

---

[1] The reader is referred for a consideration of this subject to *The Virgin Birth of Christ*, by James Orr (Hodder and Stoughton, 1907); and *The Virgin Birth*, by J. Gresham Machen (Marshall, Morgan and Scott, 1936).

'sign'. St. Paul, at the beginning of his Epistle to the Romans, writes that Jesus was 'designated Son of God in power . . . by his resurrection from the dead' (i. 4), and the earliest sermons of the apostles recorded in the Acts repeatedly assert that by the resurrection God has reversed man's sentence and vindicated His Son.

Of this resurrection St. Luke, who is known to have been an accurate and painstaking historian, says there are 'many infallible proofs' (Acts i. 3 AV). We may not feel able to go as far as Thomas Arnold who called the resurrection 'the best attested fact in history', but certainly many impartial students have judged the evidence to be extremely good. For instance, Sir Edward Clarke, K.C., wrote to the Rev. E. L. Macassey, D.D.: 'As a lawyer I have made a prolonged study of the evidences for the events of the first Easter Day. To me the evidence is conclusive, and over and over again in the High Court I have secured the verdict on evidence not nearly so compelling. Inference follows on evidence, and a truthful witness is always artless and disdains effect. The Gospel evidence for the resurrection is of this class, and as a lawyer I accept it unreservedly as the testimony of truthful men to facts they were able to substantiate.'

What is this evidence? An attempt may be made to summarize it by four statements.

I. THE SEPULCHRE WAS EMPTY

The resurrection narratives in the four Gospels begin with the visit of certain women early on Easter Sunday morning to the sepulchre. On arrival they were dumb-founded to discover that the body of the Lord had disappeared. Clearly it is a fact that the sepulchre was empty. Not many days later the apostles began to preach that Jesus had risen. It was the burden of their message. But they could hardly have expected men to believe them if a few minutes' walk could have taken them to Joseph's tomb where the body of Jesus still lay! No. The tomb was empty. The body had gone. Some explanation must be given of this fact.

First, there is the theory that the women went to the

wrong sepulchre. It was still dark, and they were dazed with sorrow. They could easily, it is claimed, have made a mistake. This sounds plausible on the surface, but it hardly bears examination. To begin with, it cannot have been completely dark. It is true that St. John says the women came 'while it was still dark' (Jn. xx. 1), but in Matthew xxviii. 1 it is 'toward the dawn', while Luke says it was 'at early dawn' (Lk. xxiv. 1), and Mark distinctly states that 'the sun had risen' (Mk. xvi. 2). Further, these women were no fools. At least two of them had seen where Joseph and Nicodemus had lain the body (Mk. xv. 47; Lk. xxiii. 55). They had even watched the whole process of burial, 'sitting opposite the sepulchre' (Mt. xxvii. 61). The same two (Mary Magdalene and Mary the mother of Joses) returned at dawn, bringing with them Salome (Mk. xvi. 1), Joanna and 'the other women' (Lk. xxiv. 10), so that if one mistook the path or the tomb, she is likely to have been corrected by the others. And if Mary Magdalene went to the wrong place the first time, she can hardly have repeated her error when she returned in the full light of morning and lingered in the garden till Jesus met her. Besides, no sentimental sorrow brought them thus early to the tomb. They were bent on a practical mission. They had bought spices and were going to complete the anointing of their Lord's body, since the approach of the sabbath had made the work so hasty two days previously. These devoted and businesslike women were not the kind to be easily deceived or to give up the task they had come to do. Again, even if they mistook the sepulchre, would Peter and John who ran to verify their story, make the same mistake, and others who doubtless came later, including Joseph and Nicodemus themselves?

Second, there is the swoon theory. Those who maintain this view would have us believe that Jesus did not die on the cross. He only fainted, they say. He then revived in the tomb, subsequently left it and made Himself known to the disciples. This theory simply bristles with problems. It is thoroughly perverse. The evidence entirely contradicts it. Pilate may have been

surprised that Jesus was already dead, but the centurion
assured him that it was so (Mk. xv. 44, 45), and Pilate
was sufficiently convinced to give Joseph permission to
remove the body from the cross. The centurion was able
to give Pilate the assurance he needed because he was
no doubt present when 'one of the soldiers pierced his
side with a spear, and at once there came out blood and
water' (Jn. xix. 34). So Joseph and Nicodemus took down
His body, wound it in the grave clothes and laid it in
Joseph's new sepulchre. Are we then seriously to believe
that Jesus was all the time only in a swoon? That after
the rigours and pains of trial, mockery, flogging and
crucifixion He could survive thirty-six hours in a stone
sepulchre with neither warmth nor food nor the tending
of His wounds? That He could then rally sufficiently to
perform the superhuman feat of shifting the boulder
which secured the mouth of the tomb, and that without
disturbing the Roman guard? That, weak and sickly and
hungry, He could appear to the disciples and give them
the impression that He had vanquished death? That He
could claim to have died and risen, could send them
into all the world and promise to be with them unto the
end of the world? That He could live somewhere for
forty days and then disappear when no one apparently
gave Him food and shelter, and no one finally saw Him
die? Such credulity is more incredible than Thomas'
unbelief.

Third, there is the notion that thieves of some kind
stole the body. There is no shred of evidence for this
conjecture. There is no explanation of how thieves could
have hoodwinked the Roman guard or moved the
boulder. Neither can one imagine why thieves should
have taken the body and left the graveclothes, nor what
possible motive they could have had for their action.

Fourth, it has been argued that the disciples themselves removed the body. This, the first evangelist tells
us, is the rumour which the Jews spread from the earliest
days. He describes how Pilate, having given permission
to Joseph to remove Christ's body, received a deputation
of chief priests and Pharisees, who said: 'Sir, we
remember how that impostor said, while he was still

alive, "After three days I will rise again." Therefore
order the sepulchre to be made secure until the third
day, lest his disciples go and steal him away, and tell
the people, "He has risen from the dead," and the last
fraud will be worse than the first.' Pilate concurred.
'Make it as secure as you can', he said, and the Jews
'made the sepulchre secure by sealing the stone and
setting a guard' (Mt. xxvii. 62-66). The first evangelist
goes on to describe how the stone, the seal and the guard
could not prevent the resurrection, and how the guard
went into the city to report to the chief priests what had
happened. After consultation they bribed the soldiers
and said, 'Tell people, "His disciples came by night and
stole him away while we were asleep." And if this comes
to the governor's ears, we will satisfy him and keep you
out of trouble.' Matthew concludes his account of this
episode with the words, 'So they took the money and did
as they were directed; and this story has been spread
among the Jews to this day' (Mt. xxviii. 11-15).

But the story does not hold water. Is it likely that a
picked guard, whether Roman or Jewish, would all sleep
on duty when detailed to watch? And if they did remain
awake, how did guileless and defenceless women get past
them and roll away the stone? Even supposing the
disciples had succeeded in removing the Lord's body,
there is a psychological factor which is hostile to the
whole theory. We learn from the first part of the Acts
that the burden of the apostolic preaching to the Jews
concerned the resurrection. 'You killed him, but God
raised him, and we are witnesses' was their refrain. Are
we then to believe that they were proclaiming what they
knew to be a deliberate lie? If they had themselves taken
Christ's body, to preach His resurrection was to spread
a known, planned falsehood. They not only preached it;
they suffered for it. They were prepared to go to prison,
to the flogging post and to death for a fairy-tale. This
does not ring true. It is so unlikely as to be almost impossible. If anything is clear from the Gospels and the Acts,
it is that the apostles were sincere. They may have been
deceived, if you like, but they were not deceivers.
Hypocrites and martyrs are not made of the same stuff.

The fifth, and perhaps the least unreasonable, human explanation of the disappearance of Christ's body is that it was taken away by the Roman or Jewish authorities. The desire to take the body into their own safe custody would have been motive enough. Needless to say, there is no more evidence for this theory than for any of the others. They are all unwarranted guesses, but this guess is less unwarrantable than the rest. However, there is one particular argument which renders it untenable. The only reason they had for taking the body would have been to forestall trickery. They had heard rumours that Christ had spoken of resurrection. They were afraid of hanky-panky. So they took the precaution of confiscating the corpse. Now, within a few weeks the apostles were boldly proclaiming that Christ had risen. The news spread rapidly. The new Nazarene movement threatened to undermine the bulwarks of Judaism and to disturb the peace of Jerusalem. The Jews feared conversions; the Romans riots. The authorities had before them one obvious course of action. They could produce the remains of the body and publish a statement of what they had done. Instead, they were silent and resorted to violence. They arrested the apostles, threatened them, flogged them, imprisoned them, vilified them, plotted against them, and killed them. But all this was entirely unnecessary if they had Christ's body. The Church was founded on the resurrection. Disprove the resurrection, and the Church would have collapsed. But they could not; the body was not in their possession. The authorities' silence is as eloquent a proof of the resurrection as the apostles' witness.

These are the theories which men have invented to try and explain the emptiness of the tomb and the disappearance of the body. None of them is satisfactory. For want therefore of any adequate alternative explanation, we may be forgiven if we prefer the biblical account of events. There is no evidence for any of these human theories. There is on the other hand a simple and sober historical narrative in the Gospels, describing the happenings of the first Easter Day. The body of Christ was not removed by men; it was raised by God.

II. THE GRAVECLOTHES WERE UNDISTURBED

It is a remarkable fact that the narratives which say that Christ's body had gone, tell us that the graveclothes had not gone. It is St. John who lays particular emphasis on this fact, for he accompanied Peter on that dramatic early morning race to the sepulchre. The account he gives of this incident (xx. 1-10) bears the unmistakable marks of first-hand experience. The evangelist is describing what he has himself witnessed. He is 'the other disciple, the one whom Jesus loved' (verse 2). He outran Peter, but did no more than look into the tomb, until Peter came and entered it. 'Then the other disciple, who reached the tomb first, also went in, and he saw and believed' (verse 8). The question is: What did he see which made him believe? The story suggests that it was not just the absence of the body, but the presence of the graveclothes and, in particular, their undisturbed condition.

The Rev. Henry Latham, formerly Master of Trinity Hall, Cambridge, has written an elaborate essay on this subject in his book, *The Risen Master* (1900), and it will be sufficient here to give a brief summary of his conclusions. Let us try to reconstruct the story. St. John tells us (xix. 38-42) that while Joseph begged Pilate for the body of Jesus, Nicodemus 'came bringing a mixture of myrrh and aloes, about a hundred pounds' weight. They took the body of Jesus, and bound it in linen cloths with the spices, as is the burial custom of the Jews'. That is to say, as they wound the linen 'bandages' round His body, they sprinkled the powdered spices into the folds. A separate cloth was no doubt used for His head as in the case of Lazarus (xi. 44). They thus enswathed His body and head, leaving His face and neck bare, according to oriental custom. They then laid the body on a stone slab which had been hewn out of the side of the cave-tomb. Now supposing we had been present in the sepulchre when the resurrection of Jesus actually took place. What should we have seen? Should we have seen Jesus begin to move, and then yawn and stretch and get up? No. We do not believe that He returned to this life. He did not recover from a swoon; He had died, and He rose again. His was a resurrection, not a resuscitation. We believe that He passed miraculously through death into an altogether new sphere of existence. What then should we have seen, had we been there? We should suddenly have noticed that the body had disappeared. It would have 'vapourized', being transmuted into something new and different and wonderful. It would have passed through the graveclothes, as it was later to pass through closed doors, leaving them untouched and almost undisturbed. Almost, but not quite. The body clothes, under the weight of 100 lbs. of spices, once the support of the body had been removed, would have subsided or collapsed, and would now be lying flat. A gap would have appeared between the body clothes and the head napkin, where His face and neck had been. And the napkin itself, because of the complicated criss-cross pattern of the bandages, might well have retained its concave shape, a crumpled turban with no head inside it.

Now a careful study of the text of St. John's narrative suggests that it is just these three characteristics of the discarded graveclothes which the beloved disciple saw. First, he saw the cloths 'lying'. The word is repeated twice (verses 5, 6) and the first time it is placed in an emphatic position in the Greek sentence. We might translate, 'He saw, as they were lying (or 'collapsed'), the linen cloths.' Next, the head napkin was 'not . . . with the linen cloths but . . . in a place by itself' (verse 7). Not that it had been bundled up and tossed into a corner. It lay still on the stone slab, but was separated from the body cloths by a noticeable space. Thirdly, this same napkin was 'not lying . . . but wrapped together . . . '. This last word Latham translates 'twirled'. The Authorized Version 'wrapped together' and the Revised Standard Version 'rolled up' are both unfortunate translations. The word aptly describes the rounded shape which the empty napkin still preserved. It is not hard to imagine the sight which greeted the eyes of the wondering apostles, as they first looked in, and then went into the tomb. The stone slab, the collapsed graveclothes, the shell of the head-cloth and the gap between the two. No wonder they 'saw and believed'. A glance at these graveclothes proved the reality, and indicated the nature, of the resurrection. They had been neither touched nor folded nor manipulated by any human being. They were like a discarded chrysalis, from which the butterfly has emerged. That they were intended to be visible, corroborative evidence for the resurrection is further suggested by the fact that, according to John, Mary Magdalene (who had returned to the tomb after bringing the news to Peter and John) 'stooped to look into the tomb; and she saw two angels in white, sitting where the body of Jesus had lain, one at the head and one at the feet' (xx. 11, 12). Presumably this means that they sat on the stone slab with the graveclothes between them. Both Matthew and Mark add that one of them said, 'He is not here; for he has risen, as he said. Come, see the place where he lay' (Mt. xxviii. 6; Mk. xvi. 6). This reference to the place where Jesus had lain, emphasized by both the position and the words of the angels, confirms the suggestion that the lie of the clothes and the absence of the body were concurrent witnesses to His resurrection.

III. THE LORD WAS SEEN

Every reader of the Gospels knows that they include some extraordinary stories of how Jesus appeared to His disciples after His resurrection. We know of ten separate appearances of the risen Lord to what Peter calls 'chosen witnesses' (Acts x. 41). It is said that He appeared to Mary Magdalene (Jn. xx. 11-18; Mk. xvi. 9), to the women returning from the sepulchre (Mt. xxviii. 9), to Peter (Lk. xxiv. 34; 1 Cor. xv. 5), to two disciples on the road to Emmaus (Lk. xxiv. 13-35; Mk. xvi. 12, 13), to the ten gathered in the upper room (Lk. xxiv. 36-42; Jn. xx. 19-23), to the eleven including Thomas (Jn. xx. 24-29; Mk. xvi. 14), to 'more than five hundred brethren at one time' probably on the mountainside in Galilee (1 Cor. xv. 6; Mt. xxviii. 16-20), to James (1 Cor. xv. 7), to some disciples including Peter, Thomas, Nathanael, James and John by the

Galilee lakeside (Jn. xxi. 1-23), and to many on the
Mount of Olives near Bethany at the time of the
ascension (Lk. xxiv. 50-53; Acts i. 6-12). St. Paul adds
himself at the end of his catalogue of those who saw
the risen Jesus (1 Cor. xv. 8), referring to his experience
on the Damascus Road, and St. Luke tells us at the
beginning of the Acts that Jesus 'presented himself alive
after his passion by many proofs, appearing to them
(i.e. the apostles) during forty days' (Acts i. 3), so that
there may well have been other appearances, of which
no record has survived.

Now we cannot lightly dismiss this body of living
testimony to the resurrection. We must find some
explanation of these narratives. Only three seem possible.
One is that they were inventions; the second that they
were hallucinations; the third that they were true.

There is no need to devote much space to the
refutation of the former suggestion. That the resurrection appearance stories are not deliberate inventions is
as plain as could be. For one thing the narratives are
sober and unadorned; for another they are graphic, and
enlivened by the detailed touches of an eyewitness. The
stories of the race to the tomb and of the walk to
Emmaus are too vivid and real to have been invented.
Besides, no one could call them good inventions. If we
had wanted to invent the resurrection, we might have
done much better ourselves. We should have been
careful to avoid the complicated jigsaw puzzle of events
which the four Gospels together produce. We should
have eliminated, or at least watered down, the doubts
and fears of the apostles. We should probably have
included a dramatic account of the resurrection itself
(as do the fantastic apocryphal Gospels), describing the
power and glory of the Son of God as He broke the
bonds of death and burst from the tomb in triumph.
But no one saw it happen, and we have no description
of it. Again, we should scarcely have chosen Mary
Magdalene as the first witness, if only to avoid Renan's
sneer that 'la passion d'une hallucinée donne au monde
un dieu ressuscité'! But there is an objection to the
theory of invention greater than the naïvety of the

narratives. It is the obvious fact, to which we have already had occasion to refer, that the apostles, and so the evangelists and the Early Church, were sublimely convinced that Jesus had risen. The whole New Testament breathes an atmosphere of certainty and conquest. Its writers may have been, if you like, tragically misled; they were definitely not deliberately misleading.

If these accounts were not inventions, were the appearances themselves hallucinations? This opinion has been widely held and confidently expressed; and of course hallucinations are not an uncommon phenomenon. A hallucination is the 'apparent perception of an external object when no such object is present' (*Shorter Oxford English Dictionary*), and is associated most frequently with someone who is at least neurotic, if not actually psychotic. Most of us have known people who see things and hear voices, and live sometimes or always in an imaginary world of their own. It is not possible to say that the disciples were unbalanced people of this type. Mary Magdalene may have been, but hardly blustering Peter and doubting Thomas.

Hallucinations have also been known to occur in quite ordinary and normal people, and in such cases two characteristics may usually be discerned. Firstly, they happen as the climax to a period of exaggerated wishful thinking. Secondly, the circumstances of time and place and mood are favourable. There must be the strong inward desire and the predisposing outward setting. When we turn to the Gospel narratives of the resurrection, however, both these factors are missing. So far from there being any sign of wishful thinking, the opposite tendency is evident. Thus, the body of Jesus was taken down from the cross, bound in graveclothes and buried in a rock-hewn, rock-closed sepulchre. The burial rites which Joseph and Nicodemus began on the Friday evening, the women came to complete on the Sunday morning. Jesus was dead and buried. They were not expecting any sequel. When they found the tomb empty, they fled in 'trembling and astonishment' and were 'afraid' (Mk. xvi. 8). When Mary Magdalene and

the other women reported that He was alive, 'they
would not believe it' (Mk. xvi. 11), and their words
'seemed to them an idle tale' (Lk. xxiv. 11). When Jesus
came and stood in their midst 'they were startled and
frightened, and supposed that they saw a spirit' (Lk.
xxiv. 37), and Jesus 'upbraided them for their unbelief
and hardness of heart' (Mk. xvi. 14). Thomas was
adamant in his refusal to believe unless he could
actually see and feel the nail-wounds (Jn. xx. 24, 25).
When later Christ met the eleven and others by
appointment on a mountain in Galilee, 'they worshipped
him; but some doubted' (Mt. xxviii. 17). Here was no
wishful thinking, no naïve credulity, no blind acceptance.
The disciples were not gullible, but rather cautious and
sceptical. They were 'foolish men, and slow of heart to
believe' (Lk. xxiv. 25). It was only through the dim
twilight of unbelief that their faith dawned at last. No
hallucination would have satisfied them; their faith was
grounded upon the hard and verifiable facts of their
personal experience.

Not only so, but the outwardly favourable circumstances were missing too. If the appearances had all
taken place in one or two particularly sacred places,
which had been hallowed by memories of Jesus, and
their mood had been expectant, our suspicions might
well be aroused. If we had only the story of the
appearances in the upper room, we should have cause
to doubt and question. If the eleven had been gathered
in that special place where Jesus had spent with them
some of His last earthly hours, and they had kept His
place vacant, and were sentimentalizing over the magic
days of the past, and had remembered His promises to
return, and had begun to wonder if He might return
and to hope that He would, until the ardour of
their expectation was consummated by His sudden
appearance, we might indeed fear that they had been
mocked by a cruel delusion. But these were not the
circumstances. Indeed, an investigation of the ten
appearances reveals an almost studied variety in the
circumstances of person, place and mood in which they
occurred. Thus, there were three individual interviews

(Mary Magdalene, Peter and James), and an interview
with two on the road to Emmaus. There were at least
ten to whom Christ appeared on the first Easter Day,
and eleven or more the following Sunday, while St.
Paul claims that more than five hundred brethren saw
Him together on one occasion (probably in Galilee). As
for places, so far from the appearances happening in one
or two sacred spots, there were almost as many places in
which He was seen as groups of people who saw Him.
There were the garden of the sepulchre, somewhere
between the garden and the city, the upper room, the
road to Emmaus, a mountain in Galilee, the lake shore
of Galilee, and the Mount of Olives near Bethany.
If there was variety in person and place, there was
variety in mood also. Mary Magdalene was weeping;
the women were afraid and astonished; Peter was full
of remorse, and Thomas of incredulity. The Emmaus
pair were distracted by the events of the week and the
disciples in Galilee by their fishing. Yet through their
doubts and fears, through their unbelief and preoccupa-
tion the risen Lord made Himself known to them. He
broke through the thick barriers of their faithlessness.
Let no man dismiss these revelations of the divine Lord
as the hallucinations of deranged, human minds.

IV. THE DISCIPLES WERE CHANGED

Perhaps the transformation of the disciples of Jesus is
the greatest evidence of all for the resurrection, because
it is entirely artless. They do not invite us to look at
themselves, as they invite us to look at the empty tomb
and the collapsed graveclothes and the Lord whom
they had seen. We can see the change in them without
being asked to look. The men who figure in the pages
of the Gospels are new men and different in the Acts.
The death of Christ left them despondent, disillusioned,
and near to despair. In the Acts they emerge as men
who hazard their lives for the name of the Lord Jesus
Christ and who turn the world upside down (Acts xv.
26, xvii. 6). What has made the change? What accounts
for their new faith and power, joy and love? Partly, no
doubt, Pentecost and the coming of the Holy Spirit; but

then the Holy Spirit came only when Jesus had risen
and ascended. It is as if the resurrection let loose mighty
moral and spiritual forces. Two examples stand out. The
first is Simon Peter. During the telling of the Passion
story Peter has faded out of the picture. He has denied
Christ three times. He has cursed and sworn as if he had
never known the sweetness of the influence of Jesus in
his life. He has gone out into the night to weep bitterly.
When Jesus is dead, he joins the others in the upper
room, behind barred doors 'for fear of the Jews' (Jn.
xx. 19), and is utterly dejected. We turn over one or two
pages in the Bible and we see him standing, probably
on the stone steps outside the same upper room of the
same house in Jerusalem, preaching so boldly and so
powerfully to a vast crowd that three thousand people
accept Christ and are baptized. We turn on to the next
chapters in the Acts and we watch him defying the very
Sanhedrin who had condemned Jesus to death, rejoicing
that he is counted worthy to suffer shame for His name,
and later sleeping in his cell on the night before his
expected execution (ii. 14-41, iv. 1-22, v. 41, xii. 1-6).
Simon Peter is a new man. The shifting sands have
been blown away; true to his nickname, he is a real
rock now. What has made the difference?

Or take James, who later assumed a position of
leadership in the Jerusalem Church. He is one of 'the
brethren of the Lord', who throughout the Gospels are
represented as not believing in Jesus. 'Even his brothers
did not believe in him' (Jn. vii. 5). But when we reach
the first chapter of the Acts, the list which St. Luke
gives of the assembled disciples concludes with the
words 'and . . . his brothers' (verse 14). James is evidently
a believer now. What has made the difference? What
convinced him? Perhaps we have the clue we are seeking
in 1 Cor. xv. 7 where St. Paul, cataloguing those who
had seen the risen Jesus, adds 'he appeared to James'.

It was the resurrection which transformed Peter's
fear into courage, and James' doubt into faith. It was
the resurrection which changed the sabbath into Sunday
and the Jewish remnant into the Christian Church. It
was the resurrection which changed Saul the Pharisee

into Paul the apostle, and turned his persecuting into preaching.

These are the evidences for the resurrection. If the sepulchre was empty and the graveclothes remained undisturbed; if the Lord was seen and the disciples were changed, there is no other explanation than the great Christian affirmation 'the Lord is risen indeed'.

*　　　*　　　*

We have been occupied for three chapters in a critical investigation of the most absorbing personality of history, a modest carpenter from Nazareth, who became a peasant preacher and died a felon's death. His claims were stupendous. He seems to have been morally perfect. He rose from the dead. The cumulative weight of this evidence is all but conclusive. It only requires that short step of faith which brings us to our knees before Him and puts on our lips the mighty confession of a doubting Thomas, 'My Lord and my God.' To deny that 'Jesus is the Christ come in the flesh' is to be or to follow Antichrist (1 Jn. ii. 22, iv. 2, 3; 2 Jn. 7). To believe it, or rather to believe Him, is to receive eternal life (Jn. xx. 31).

II. MAN'S NEED

CHAPTER V

THE FACT AND NATURE OF SIN

WE have devoted considerable space to an examination of the evidence for Jesus Christ's unique deity; and we may be convinced that He is the Lord, the Son of God. Yet in the New Testament it is not His person only which is described, but also His work. The New Testament authors are occupied not just with who He was, but with what He did. He is therefore presented not simply as the Lord who came from heaven but as the Saviour who died on a cross. Not that the two can be separated; they are closely linked. Indeed the validity of His work depends on the divinity of His person.

But in order to appreciate the work which He accomplished, we must understand who we are as well as who He is. His work was done for us. It was the work of a person for persons. It was a work undertaken for needy persons by the only person competent to meet their need. His competence lies in His deity; our need lies in our sin. We have tested His competence; we must now expose our need.

So we turn from Christ to man, from the sinlessness and glory that are in Him to the sin and shame that are in us. Only then, after we have clearly grasped what we are, shall we be in a position to perceive the wonder of what He has done for us and offers to us. Only when we have had the malady accurately diagnosed, shall we be willing to take the medicine prescribed.

Sin is an unpopular subject, and Christians are often

criticized for harping too much upon it. But it is only
because Christians are realists that they do so. Sin is
not a convenient invention of parsons to keep them in
their job; it is a universal fact. The biblical writers are
quite clear about this. 'There is no man who does not
sin,' says Solomon in an aside during his great prayer
at the dedication of the Temple (1 Ki. viii. 46). 'Surely
there is not a righteous man on earth who does good
and never sins' adds the Preacher in the Book of
Ecclesiastes (vii. 20). Several of the Psalms lament the
universality of human sin. Psalm xiv, which describes
the godless 'fool', gives a very pessimistic description of
human wickedness: 'They are corrupt, they do abomin-
able deeds, there is none that does good. The Lord looks
down from heaven upon the children of men, to see if
there are any that act wisely, that seek after God. They
have all gone astray, they are all alike corrupt; there is
none that does good, no, not one' (verses 1-3). The
Psalmist's conscience tells him that if God were to rise
up in judgment against man, none could escape His
condemnation. 'If thou, O Lord, shouldst mark
iniquities, Lord, who could stand?' (Ps. cxxx. 3). So he
prays, 'Enter not into judgment with thy servant; for
no man living is righteous before thee' (Ps. cxliii. 2). The
prophets are as insistent as the psalmists on the fact that
all men are sinners, and no statements are more definite
than the two which are to be found in the second half
of the Book of Isaiah. 'All we like sheep have gone
astray; we have turned every one to his own way' (liii.
6), and 'We have all become like one who is unclean,
and all our righteous deeds are like a polluted garment'
(lxiv. 6).

Nor is this a fancy of Old Testament writers. St. Paul
opens his Epistle to the Romans by arguing elaborately
for nearly the first three chapters that all men indis-
criminately, whether Jews or Gentiles, are sinners in
God's sight. He describes in vivid terms the degraded
morals of the pagan world and adds that the Jew is no
better, since, possessing God's holy law himself and
teaching it to others, he is yet guilty of breaking it. The
apostle then quotes from the Psalms and the prophet

Isaiah to illustrate his theme, and concludes, 'there is no distinction; since all have sinned and fall short of the glory of God' (iii. 22, 23). St. John is, if anything, even more explicit when he declares that 'If we say that we have no sin, we deceive ourselves', and 'If we say we have not sinned, we make him a liar' (1 Jn. i. 8, 10).

The universal extent of human sin is, however, not a truth which can be known only by revelation. It is a fact of our own everyday experience. We see it as we read history or the newspapers. We see it as we travel abroad or mix with our fellow men. We see it in our own home. We see it in our own lives. Nearly all our legislation, whether in law or bye-law, has grown up because human beings cannot be trusted to settle their disputes with honesty and without self-interest. Many of the happenings of civilized society would not exist if it were not for human sin. A promise is not enough; we need a contract. Doors are not enough; we have to lock and bolt them. The payment of fares is not enough; we have to be issued with tickets which are punched, inspected and collected. Law and order are not enough; we need the police to enforce them. All these things, and many others, to which we have grown so accustomed that we take them for granted, are due to our sin. We cannot trust each other. We need protection against one another. It is a sorry state of affairs.

But what is sin? Its universal extent is clear; what is its nature? Several words are used in the Bible to describe it. They group themselves into two categories, according to whether wrongdoing is regarded negatively or positively. Negatively, it is shortcoming. One word represents it as a lapse, a slip, a blunder. Another pictures it as the failure to hit a mark, as when throwing a spear at a target. Yet another shows it to be an inward badness, a disposition which falls short of what is good. Positively, sin is transgression. One word makes sin the trespass of a boundary. Another reveals it as lawlessness. Yet another as an act which violates justice. Both these groups of words imply the existence of a moral standard. It is either an ideal which we fail to reach, or a law which we break. 'Whoever knows what is right to do and fails to do it, for him it is sin' (Jas. iv. 17). That is the negative aspect. 'Every one who commits sin is guilty of lawlessness; sin is lawlessness' (1 Jn. iii. 4). That is the positive aspect.

The Bible accepts the fact that men have different standards. The Jews have the law of Moses. The Gentiles have the law of conscience. But all men have fallen short of their standard. All men have broken their law. It is the same for us. What is our ethical code? It may be the law of Moses or the law of Jesus. It may be public school morality, or a white man's taboos, or the conventions of the decent chap. It may be the Buddhist's noble eightfold path or the Muslim's five pillars of conduct. But whatever it is, we have not succeeded in observing it. We all stand self-condemned. To some good-living people this comes as a genuine surprise. They have their ideals and think they attain them more or less. They do not indulge in much introspection. They are not unduly self-critical. They know they have had occasional lapses. They are aware of certain character deficiencies. But they are not particularly alarmed by them and consider themselves no worse than the rest of men. All this is understandable enough, until we remember two things. Firstly, our sense of failure depends on how high our standards are. It is quite easy to consider oneself good at high jumping if the bar is never raised above 3 ft. 6 in. Secondly, God concerns Himself with the thought behind the deed and with the motive behind the action. Jesus clearly taught this in the sermon on the mount, and we shall need to take it into consideration. With these two principles in mind, it will be a healthy exercise to take the Ten Commandments as our standard and see how very far short of it every man falls.

THE TEN COMMANDMENTS
(Ex. xx. 1-17)

1. 'You shall have no other gods before me.'
This is God's demand for man's exclusive worship. It is not necessary to worship the sun, the moon and the stars to break this law. We break it whenever we give to

something or someone the first place in our thoughts or our affections. It may be some engrossing sport or absorbing hobby. It may be someone whom we idolize. It may be some selfish ambition which engages all our attention and consumes all our energies. We may worship a god of gold and silver in the form of safe investments and a healthy bank balance. We may worship a god of wood and stone in the form of property, always wanting a bigger and better house or car or television set. None of these things is wrong in itself. It only becomes wrong when we give to it the place in our lives which is due only to God. Sin is fundamentally the exaltation of self at the expense of God. What someone wrote of the Englishman is true of everyman that he is 'a self-made man who worships his creator'. For us to keep this first commandment would be, as Jesus said, to love the Lord our God with all our heart and with all our soul and with all our mind (Mt. xxii. 37); to see all things from His point of view and do nothing without reference to Him; to make His will our guide and His glory our goal; to put Him first in thought, word and deed; in business and leisure; in friendships and career; in the use of our money, time and talents; at work and at home. No man has ever kept this commandment except Jesus of Nazareth.

2. *'You shall not make yourself a graven image.'*

If the first commandment concerns the object of our worship, the second concerns its manner. The first commandment proclaims God's unity; the second His spirituality. In the first commandment God demands our exclusive, and in the second our sincere and spiritual, worship, for 'God is spirit, and those who worship him must worship in spirit and truth' (Jn. iv. 24). We may never have manufactured some gruesome metal image with our hands, but what hideous mental image do we hold in our minds? Further, although this commandment does not forbid the use of all external forms in worship, it implies that they too are useless unless there is inward reality also. We may have attended church; have we ever really worshipped God? We may have said prayers; have we ever really prayed? We may have read the Bible; have we ever let God speak to us through it and done what He said? It is no good approaching God with our lips, if our hearts are far from Him (Is. xxix. 13; Mk. vii. 6). This is the sin of the backsliding Jew, of the Pharisee, even of the idolator. This is the prizing of external religious objects and acts, when there is no inward sincerity. This is humbug.

3. 'You shall not take the name of the Lord your God in vain.'

The name of God represents the nature of God. There is much in the Bible which commands us to reverence His name, and in the Lord's Prayer we constantly pray that His name may be hallowed. His holy name can be profaned by our loose language, and most of us could do worse than revise our vocabulary from time to time. But to take God's name in vain is not just a matter of words, but also of thoughts and deeds. Whenever our behaviour is inconsistent with our belief, or our practice contradicts our preaching, we take God's name in vain. To call God 'Lord' and disobey Him is to take His name in vain. To call God 'Father' and be filled with anxiety and doubts is to deny His name. To take God's name in vain is to talk one way and act another. This is hypocrisy.

4. 'Remember the sabbath day, to keep it holy.'

The Jews' sabbath and the Christians' Sunday are a divine institution. To set one day in seven apart is not just a human arrangement or a social convenience. It is God's plan. He made the sabbath for man (Mk. ii. 27), and since He also made the man for whom He made the sabbath, He adapted it to man's need. Man's body and mind need rest, and man's spirit needs the opportunity for worship. The sabbath is therefore a day of rest and a day of worship. How few of us observe it as such! Not only do we often work ourselves, but we engage in such pursuits as give other people unnecessary work and so deny them and us the opportunity we need for the worship of God. The commandment requires us to work six days and to rest on the seventh. It is our duty to see that others for whom we are responsible (our family, our domestic staff, our employees) are free to rest and to worship also. Sunday is a 'holy' day, set apart for God. It is the Lord's day and not our day. It is therefore to be spent in His way and not in ours, for His worship and His service and not just for our selfish pleasure.

5. 'Honour your father and your mother.'

This fifth commandment, setting forth our duty to our parents, yet belongs to the first table of the law, which concerns our duty to God, because our parents, at least during our minority, stand towards us *in loco Dei*. They represent God's authority. And yet it is in his own home that a young person is often most selfish and inconsiderate. He is not on show there to the outside world. He appears in his true colours. 'Disobedient to their parents' is one of the descriptions which St. Paul gives of the men who will abound in the last days (2 Tim. iii. 2), and it is often in this realm that our innate selfishness is revealed, even when we have attained our majority. It is all too easy to be ungrateful and neglectful, and to fail to show them the respect and affection they deserve. How often do we write to them or visit them? Or do they need financial support which we could give but deny them?

6. 'You shall not kill.'

This commandment is not just a prohibition of actual murder. If looks could kill, many would kill with a look. If murder can be committed by cutting words, many are guilty. Indeed Jesus said that to be angry with someone and to be insulting is just as serious (Mt. v. 21-26), and St. John draws the right conclusion when he writes, 'Any one who hates his brother is a murderer' (1 Jn. iii. 15). Every loss of temper, every outburst of uncontrolled passion, every stirring of sullen rage, every bitter resentment and thirsting for revenge—all these things are murder. We can kill by malicious gossip. We can kill by studied neglect and cruelty. We can kill by spite and jealousy. We have probably all done so.

7. 'You shall not commit adultery.'

Again, this commandment has a far wider application than merely to unfaithfulness in marriage. It includes fornication before marriage. It includes all those relaxations of strict morality which we gloss over by euphemisms. It includes having a honeymoon while you're engaged, indiscriminate flirting, 'adventure' and 'experimenting'. It includes all solitary sexual experience. It includes all sexual perversions, for even if men or women are not responsible for the perverted instinct, they are for its indulgence. It includes selfish demands within wedlock, and many, if not all, divorces. It includes the deliberate reading of suggestive literature, and the gratification of impure thoughts. Jesus made this clear also when He said, ' . . . every one who looks at a woman lustfully has already committed adultery with her in his heart' (Mt. v. 28). Just as to entertain murderous thoughts in the heart is to commit murder, so to entertain adulterous thoughts in the heart is to commit adultery. This commandment in fact embraces every abuse of a noble power given by God, and every debasement of what is His sacred and beautiful gift.

8. 'You shall not steal.'

To steal is to rob a person of anything which belongs to him or is due to him. The theft of money or property is not the only infringement of this commandment. Tax evasion is robbery. So is dodging the customs. So is working short hours. When the world says 'finding's keeping', God says it is stealing. What the world calls 'scrounging' God calls stealing. To overwork and underpay one's staff is to break this commandment. There must be few of us, if any, who have been consistently and scrupulously honest in personal and business affairs. As Arthur Hugh Clough wrote:

'Thou shalt not kill', but need'st not strive
  Officiously to keep alive:
'Thou shalt not steal',—an empty feat
  When it's more lucrative to cheat.

Moreover, these negative commandments all have a positive counterpart. In order truly to abstain from killing, one must do all in one's power to foster the health and preserve the life of others. To refrain from the act of adultery is insufficient. The commandment requires the right, healthy and honourable attitude of each sex towards the other. To avoid stealing is not very virtuous, if one is niggardly and miserly and mean. According to the Scottish Shorter Catechism, this eighth commandment requires that 'in every lawful way we should procure and further the wealth and outward estate of others'. And St. Paul was not satisfied that a thief should stop stealing. He had to start working. Indeed, he had to continue in honest labour until he found himself able to give to those in need (Eph. iv. 28). From a burglar to a benefactor!

9. *'You shall not bear false witness against your neighbour.'*

The last five commandments display that respect for the rights of the individual which is true love. To break these commandments is to rob a man of the things most precious to him, his life ('you shall not kill'), his home and his honour ('you shall not commit adultery'), his property ('you shall not steal'), and now his reputation ('you shall not bear false witness against your neighbour'). This commandment is not only applicable to the lawcourts. It does include perjury. But it also includes all forms of scandal and slander, all idle talk and tittle-tattle, all lies and deliberate exaggerations or distortions of the truth. We can bear false witness by listening to unkind rumours as well as by passing them on, by making jokes at somebody else's expense, by creating false impressions, by not correcting untrue statements, and by our silence as well as by our speech.

10. 'You shall not covet.'

The tenth commandment is in some ways the most revealing of all. It lifts the decalogue from the realm of a civil law into the realm of a personal ethic. It makes it not just an outward legal code but an inward moral standard. The civil law cannot touch us for covetousness. Covetousness belongs to the inner life. It lurks in the heart and in the mind, and the civil law is therefore not interested in covetousness unless it breaks out into an act of stealing. What lust is to adultery and what temper is to murder, that covetousness is to theft. The particular things which we are not to covet and which are mentioned in the commandment are surprisingly modern. In these days of housing and staff shortage there is much coveting of our neighbour's house and servants; and the divorce courts would not be so full if men did not covet their neighbour's wife. 'Covetousness . . . is idolatry' wrote St. Paul (Col. iii. 5), and by contrast, 'There is great gain in godliness with contentment' (1 Tim. vi. 6).

A rehearsal of these commandments has brought to light an ugly catalogue of sins. So much takes place beneath the surface of our lives, in the secret places of our minds, which the world does not see and which we manage even to conceal from ourselves. But God sees these things. His eye penetrates into the deep recesses of our hearts. 'Before him no creature is hidden, but all are open and laid bare to the eyes of him with whom we have to do' (Heb. iv. 13). He sees us as we really are, and His law reveals the serious extent of our sins. Indeed, it was the purpose of the law to expose sin, for 'through the law comes knowledge of sin' (Rom. iii. 20).

When C. H. Spurgeon, later to be the prince of Baptist preachers, was only fourteen years old, a conviction of sin, which had begun when he was only ten, rushed in full flood over him. Two related ideas filled him with dread and penitence: 'God's majesty and my sinfulness.' He had a crushing sense of his unworthiness. 'I do not hesitate to say that those who examined my life would not have seen any extraordinary sin, yet as I

looked upon *myself* I saw outrageous sin against God.
I was not like other boys, untruthful, dishonest, swearing
and so on. But of a sudden, I met Moses carrying the
law . . . God's Ten Words . . . and as I read them,
they all seemed to join in condemning me in the sight
of the thrice holy Jehovah.' In our case, too, nothing
can convince us of our sinfulness like the lofty, righteous
law of God.

CHAPTER VI

THE CONSEQUENCES OF SIN

WE have indicated the universality of human sin and sought to exhibit its nature by reference to the ten commandments. We should like to leave this distasteful subject and pass on immediately to the good news of Christ's salvation, but we are not quite ready to do so. Another aspect of sin must be reviewed before we are in a position to appreciate what God has done for us and is offering to us in Christ. This concerns the fruits of sin. Sin may be a fact, and that a universal fact; but is it a very serious fact? What are its chief consequences? The evil results of sin can best be understood when its effect is seen upon God, upon ourselves and upon our fellow men.

I. ALIENATION FROM GOD

Perhaps the most dreadful of all sin's consequences is that it estranges us from God. Man's highest destiny is to know God and to be in personal relationship with God. Man's chief claim to nobility is that he was made in the image of God and is therefore capable of knowing Him. But this God whom we are meant to know and whom we ought to know is a moral Being. He is infinite in all His moral perfections. He is a holy God. He is a pure and righteous God. He is ' . . . the high and lofty One who inhabits eternity, whose name is Holy'; He 'dwells in unapproachable light' (Is. lvii. 15; 1 Tim. vi. 16). Indeed ' . . . God is light and in him is no darkness at all' so that 'If we say we have fellowship with him while we walk in darkness, we lie and do not live according to the truth' (1 Jn. i. 5, 6). ' . . . our God is a consuming fire' (Heb. xii. 29; Dt. iv. 24). 'Who among us can dwell with the devouring fire? Who among us can dwell with everlasting burnings?' (Is. xxxiii. 14).

'Thou . . . art of purer eyes than to behold evil and canst not look on wrong' (Hab. i. 13).

All those men of God in the Bible who have caught a glimpse of God's glory have shrunk from the sight in an overwhelming consciousness of their own sins. Moses, to whom God appeared in the bush that burned but was not consumed, 'hid his face, for he was afraid to look at God.' Job, to whom God spoke 'out of the whirlwind' in words which exalted His transcendent majesty, cried out, 'I had heard of thee by the hearing of the ear, but now my eye sees thee; therefore I despise myself, and repent in dust and ashes.' Isaiah, a young man at the threshold of his career, had a vision of God as the King of Israel 'sitting upon a throne, high and lifted up', surrounded by worshipping angels who sang of His holiness and glory, and he said, 'Woe is me! For I am lost; for I am a man of unclean lips, and I dwell in the midst of a people of unclean lips; for my eyes have seen the King, the Lord of hosts!' When Ezekiel received his strange vision of living winged creatures and whirring wheels, and above them a throne, and on the throne One like a man, enveloped in the brightness of fire and of the rainbow, he recognized it as 'the appearance of the likeness of the glory of the Lord', and he added, 'When I saw it, I fell upon my face.' Saul of Tarsus, travelling to Damascus, mad with rage against the Christians, was struck to the ground and blinded by a brilliant light which flashed from heaven more brightly than the noonday sun, and wrote later of his vision of the risen Christ, 'He appeared also to me.' The aged John, exiled on the island of Patmos, describes in detail his vision of the risen and glorified Jesus, whose 'eyes were like a flame of fire' and whose 'face was like the sun shining in full strength', and he tells us, 'When I saw him, I fell at his feet as though dead.'[1]

If the curtain which veils the unspeakable majesty of God could be drawn aside but for a moment, we too should not be able to bear the sight. As it is, we only

[1] See Ex. iii. 1-6; Jb. xlii. 5, 6; Is. vi. 1-5; Ezk. i. 26-28; Acts ix. 1-9; 1 Cor. xv. 8; Rev. i. 9-17.

dimly perceive how pure and brilliant must be the glory of almighty God. However, we know enough to realize that sinful man while still in his sins can never approach this holy God. A great chasm yawns between God in His righteousness and man in his sin. 'What partnership have righteousness and iniquity? Or what fellowship has light with darkness?' (2 Cor. vi. 14). That sin cuts us off from God is seen illustrated in the construction of both the Tabernacle and the Temple. Both were made in two compartments, the first and larger being called the Holy Place, and the further and smaller being called the Most Holy Place or the Holy of Holies. In this inner sanctuary was the Shekinah glory, the visible symbol of God's presence. Between the two was the 'veil', a thick curtain which barred access into the Holy of Holies. No one might pass through into God's presence, except the high priest, and he only on the annual Day of Atonement and then only if he took with him the blood of a sacrifice for sins. What was thus visibly demonstrated to the Israelites is taught by Old and New Testament writers. Sin brings inevitable separation, and this separation is 'death', spiritual death, the severance of the soul from God, its only life. 'The wages of sin is death' (Rom. vi. 23). Further, if the soul in this world rejects Jesus Christ through whom alone it may find eternal life, it will die eternally in the next world. Hell is a grim and dreadful reality. Let no man deceive you. Jesus Himself spoke of it. He often called it 'outer darkness' (e.g. Mt. xxv. 30), because it is infinite separation from God who is light. It is also called in the Bible 'the second death' and 'the lake of fire', terms which describe (no doubt symbolically) the forfeiture of eternal life and the ghastly thirst of the soul which are involved in irrevocable banishment from God's presence (e.g. Rev. xx. 14, 15; cf. Lk. xvi. 19-31).

This separation from God which is caused by sin is not only taught in the Bible; it is confirmed by human experience. I can still remember my own perplexity when as a boy I said my prayers and tried to penetrate into God's presence. I could not understand why God seemed shrouded in mists and I could not come near

Him. He seemed very, very far away. I know the reason now. Isaiah has given me the answer. 'Behold the Lord's hand is not shortened, that it cannot save, or his ear dull, that it cannot hear; but your iniquities have made a separation between you and your God, and your sins have hid his face from you so that he does not hear' (Is. lix. 1, 2). We are tempted to say to God, as in Lamentations (iii. 44), 'Thou hast wrapped thyself with a cloud so that no prayer can pass through.' But in fact God is not responsible for the cloud. We are. Our sins blot out God's face from us as effectively as the clouds do the sun. Many people have confessed to me that they have had the same desolate experience. Sometimes, in emergencies, in danger, in joy or in the contemplation of beauty, God seems to them to be near, but more often than not they are aware of an inexplicable awayness from God, and their soul feels abandoned. This is not just a feeling; it is a fact. Until our sins are cleansed away, we are exiles. Our soul is lost. We have no communion with God. We are 'dead through the trespasses and sins' (Eph. ii. 1) which we have committed.

It is this that accounts for the restlessness of men and women today. There is a hunger in people's hearts which nothing can satisfy but God Himself. There is a vacuum in man's soul which only God can fill. The demand for sensational news in the Press and for extravagant love or crime stories at the pictures; pools and pubs; the dirt track and the dog track; the forest of television aerials in built-up areas—all these things are signs of man's search for satisfaction. Some of these things may be perfectly innocent in themselves. It is the exaggerated importance they are given in the lives of millions which betrays man's thirst for, and separation from, God. St. Augustine was right in the oft-quoted words which come near the beginning of his *Confessions:* 'Thou hast made us for Thyself, and our hearts are restless till they rest in Thee.' This situation is tragic beyond words. Man is missing the destiny for which God made him.

II. BONDAGE TO SELF

Sin does not only estrange; it enslaves. It not only

alienates us from God; it brings us into captivity. We need now to consider the inwardness of sin. Sin is not merely an unfortunate outward act or habit; it is a deep-seated inward corruption. The sins we commit are merely outward and visible expressions of this inward and invisible malady. Jesus explained that just as the character of the fruit depends on the character of the tree, so our actions are determined by our hearts. It is out of the heart that the mouth speaks (Mt. xii. 33-35). Similarly, we might say that it is not the spots which constitute the measles. The spots are only the symptoms of a disease which has invaded the system. Our sins are symptoms too. They reveal a spiritual disease, a disease which grips the very heart of man. 'The heart is deceitful above all things, and desperately corrupt; who can understand it?' (Je. xvii. 9). And Jesus said, 'From within, out of the heart of man, come evil thoughts, fornication, theft, murder, adultery, coveting, wickedness, deceit, licentiousness. . . . All these evil things come from within, and they defile a man' (Mk. vii. 21-23). The Bible is full of references to this infection of human nature. It is what theologians mean by 'original sin'. 'Original Sin . . . is the fault and corruption of the Nature of every man. . . . And this infection of nature doth remain. . . .'[1] It is a tendency or bias towards sin and self-centredness, which we inherit, which is rooted deeply in our human personality, and which manifests itself in a thousand ugly ways. St. Paul called it 'the flesh', and gives an inventory of its 'works', or products. 'Now the works of the flesh are plain: immorality, impurity, licentiousness, idolatry, sorcery, enmity, strife, jealousy, anger, selfishness, dissension, party spirit, envy, drunkenness, carousing, and the like' (Gal. v. 19-21).

It is because sin is an inward corruption of human nature that we are in bondage. It is not so much certain acts or habits which enslave us, but the evil infection from which these spring. Many times in the New Testament men are described as 'slaves'. It is a designation we resent, but it is accurate. Jesus aroused the

---

[1] Article IX of Articles of Religion of the Church of England

indignation of certain Pharisees when He said to them, 'If you continue in my word, you are truly my disciples, and you will know the truth, and the truth will make you free.' They retorted, 'We are descendants of Abraham, and have never been in bondage to anyone. How is it that you say, "You will be made free"?' Jesus answered them, 'Truly, truly, I say to you, every one who commits sin is a slave to sin' (Jn. viii. 31-34). St. Paul several times in his Epistles describes realistically the humiliating servitude into which sin brings us. 'You . . . were once slaves of sin' (Rom. vi. 17). ' . . . We all once lived in the passions of our flesh, following the desires of body and mind' (Eph. ii. 3). 'We ourselves were once foolish, disobedient, led astray, slaves to various passions and pleasures' (Tit. iii. 3). The example of our lack of self-mastery which James gives is the difficulty we have in controlling our tongue. In a well-known chapter full of graphic metaphor he says that if a man 'makes no mistakes in what he says he is a perfect man, able to bridle the whole body also'. He points out that 'the tongue is a little member and boasts of great things'. Its influence spreads like fire; it 'is a restless evil' and is 'full of deadly poison'. We can tame all kinds of beasts and birds, 'but no human being can tame the tongue' (Jas. iii. 1-12).

We know this only too well. We have high ideals but weak wills. We want to live a good life, but we are chained and imprisoned. We are not free. We are slaves. We come in tears to God and say:

> 'It is not finished Lord,
> There is not one thing done,
> There is no battle of my life,
> That I have really won.
> And now I come to tell Thee
> How I fought to fail,
> My human, all too human, tale
> Of weakness and futility.'[1]

It is no good giving us rules of conduct; we cannot keep them. Let God go on saying 'Thou shalt not', yet we

[1] Studdert Kennedy.

shall to the end of time. We do not need a lecture; we need a Saviour. It is not the education of the mind only which can help; it is a change of heart. Man needs power, not advice. He has found the secret of physical power. His discoveries in the realm of atomic physics are spreading alarm throughout the world. Now man needs spiritual power, power to set him free from himself, power to conquer and control himself, power to give him moral character to match his scientific achievement.

III. CONFLICT WITH OTHERS

Still our list of the dreadful consequences of sin is not finished. There is one more fact to consider. We have seen that sin is a deep-seated infection of nature. It lies at the root of man's personality. It controls his ego. In fact, sin is self. And all our sins are therefore assertions of the self against either God or man. The ten commandments, although a series of negative prohibitions, set forth our duty to God and to others. This is even more clear in the positive summary of the law which Jesus made by joining a verse from Leviticus (xix. 18) to a verse from Deuteronomy (vi. 5): 'You shall love the Lord your God with all your heart, and with all your soul, and with all your mind. This is the great and first commandment. And a second is like it, You shall love your neighbour as yourself. On these two commandments depend all the law and the prophets' (Mt. xxii. 37-40). It is important to observe that the first commandment concerns our duty to God, and not our duty to our neighbour. We are to love God first; and then we are to love our neighbour as ourselves. Sin is the reversal of this order. We put ourselves first, our neighbour next, and God somewhere in the background. The man who recently wrote his autobiography and entitled it *Dear Me*[1] was only giving expression to what we all think of ourselves. When the ice-cream is brought into a children's party or the cricket bat is produced before a game, there is an uninhibited chorus of 'Me first!'. As we grow up.

[1] *Dear Me*, by A. S. Turnbull (Macmillan).

we learn not to say that kind of thing; but we still think it. Archbishop William Temple's definition of original sin perfectly describes this truth : 'I am the centre of the world I see; where the horizon is depends on where I stand. . . . Education may make my self-centredness less disastrous by widening my horizon of interest; so far it is like climbing a tower, which widens the horizon for physical vision, while leaving me still the centre and standard of reference.'[1]

Now our self-centredness does not only manifest itself against God. It also reveals itself against our fellows. Sir Sidney Smith, Dean of the Faculty of Medicine at the University of Edinburgh, says that a child comes into the world aggressive, acquisitive, and in all ways a potential criminal. *Watchman,* who repeated this statement in the *Church of England Newspaper* (31 July 1953) adds 'in my youth I was taught to call this original sin, Sir Sidney'! The problem of human relationships is as common now as it ever was. We never find it easy to take a back seat, or play second fiddle to somebody else. We always want to be the top dog. We sometimes catch ourselves out when we are not thinking. When the meal is being served, we put the first plate down in front of ourselves, and forget to pass it on. We get on with our own meal and are more keen on looking after ourselves than our neighbour. We would not mind jumping a queue if we could avoid being detected. We find it easier to talk than to listen, easier to receive than to give.

Yes, the motive of self-interest is very prominent in all our behaviour. Either we have superiority or inferiority feelings. We do not adjust ourselves easily to others. We may have too high an opinion of ourselves or too low an opinion. In the latter case we usually hope that other people will notice our humility. We seldom have what St. Paul called 'a sober judgment' of ourselves (Rom. xii. 3). Some of us are sensitive and prickly; others are jealous and resentful, contemptuous or thoughtless. All the relationships of life are complicated

[1] *Christianity and the Social Order,* pp. 36-37.

—parents and children, husband and wife, employer and employed. Juvenile delinquency no doubt has many causes, and much is due to lack of security in the home; but the fact is that delinquents are (for whatever reason) asserting themselves against society. Hundreds of divorces could be prevented if people were humble enough to blame themselves more than their partner. Whenever couples have been to see me because their marriage was threatened, I have noticed that each tells a different story—a story sometimes so different that one would not guess they described the same situation unless one knew. Most quarrels are due to a misunderstanding, and the misunderstanding is due to our failure to appreciate the other man's point of view. This is true in industrial disputes as much as in domestic quarrels. Many management-worker conflicts could be resolved if both sides first examined themselves critically and then examined the other side charitably, instead of which we are always charitable to ourselves and critical of others. The same could be said of complex international unrest. The tensions of today are due largely to fear and folly. Our outlook is onesided. We exaggerate our virtue and the other man's vice.

It is easy to write this condemnation of social relationships today. The only reason for doing so is to show how human sin or self-centredness is the cause of all our troubles. It brings us into conflict with each other. If only the spirit of self-assertion could be replaced by the spirit of self-sacrifice, our conflicts would cease. And self-sacrifice is called in the Bible 'love'. While sin is possessive, love is expansive. Sin's characteristic is the desire to get. Love's characteristic is the desire to give.

> 'Love ever gives,
> Forgives, outlives,
> And ever stands with open hands
> And while it lives it gives.
> For this is love's prerogative
> To give—and give—and give.'

What man needs is a radical change of nature, what

Professor H. M. Gwatkin called 'a change from self to unself'. Man cannot work it within himself. He cannot operate on himself. Again, he needs a Saviour.

This exposure of our sin has only one purpose. It is to convince us of our need of Jesus Christ, and to prepare us for an understanding and an acceptance of what He offers. Faith is born of need. We shall never accept Christ unless we feel our need of Him. He said Himself, 'Those who are well have no need of a physician, but those who are sick; I came not to call the righteous, but sinners' (Mk. ii. 17). Only when we have realized and admitted our sickness and its gravity, shall we admit our desperate need of the soul's Physician. Christianity is a rescue religion. People do not appreciate it unless they know they need to be rescued.

In the next two chapters we shall see how God has taken the initiative in Christ to solve man's problem, his sin. We shall see how the three grim consequences of our sins can be overcome through Jesus Christ. He died for our sins to end our alienation and bring us back to God. He rose again and sent the Holy Spirit that men might be born again, receive a new nature and be set free from the bondage of their sins. He founded a world-wide brotherhood, the Christian Church, in which His people are bound together by the cords of love.

III. CHRIST'S WORK

CHAPTER VII

THE DEATH OF CHRIST

IF man is a sinner, he needs a Saviour, and it was primarily to fulfil this rôle that Jesus Christ came. 'The Father has sent his Son as the Saviour of the world' (1 Jn. iv. 14). Indeed, none but the Son of God could be the Saviour of men. How He has accomplished this salvation it will be our purpose in this chapter and the next to discover.

Salvation means deliverance from sin, and because sin has three principal consequences, as we have seen, salvation includes the liberation of man from them all. Through Jesus Christ our Saviour we can be recalled from banishment, and reconciled to God the Father in heaven. We can be set free from our moral bondage; and we can have the old discords replaced by a fellowship of love. The first aspect of salvation Christ made possible by His suffering of death, the second by the gift of His Spirit and the third by the building of His Church. The first will occupy our thought in this chapter; the second and third in the next.

St. Paul described his work as a 'ministry of reconciliation' (2 Cor. v. 18) and his gospel as a 'message of reconciliation' (v. 19). Moreover, he makes it quite clear in the same passage whence this reconciliation springs. God is its author, he says, and Christ its agent. 'All this is from God, who through Christ reconciled us to himself' (v. 18). Again, 'God was in Christ reconciling the world to himself' (v. 19). What was wrought out through the body of Jesus in death on a cross had its

83

origin in the mind and heart of the eternal God. No
explanation of Christ's death or man's salvation which
fails to do justice to this fact is loyal to the teaching of
the Bible. 'God so loved the world that he gave his
only Son, that whoever believes in him should not perish
but have eternal life' (Jn. iii. 16). When the apostle Paul
writes about the reconciliation of the sinner to God, he
is consistent in his use of language. What God plans,
Christ effects through His death, 'for in him all the
fulness of God was pleased to dwell, and through him
to reconcile to himself all things, whether on earth or
in heaven, making peace by the blood of his cross' (Col.
i. 19, 20). It is this same word 'reconciliation' which in
Romans v. 11 is translated in the Authorized Version
'atonement'. The English term 'atonement' denotes an
action by which two conflicting parts are made 'at one',
or the state in which their oneness is enjoyed and
expressed. This 'atonement', writes St. Paul in this
passage, we have 'received' through our Lord and
Saviour Jesus Christ. We have not ourselves achieved
it by our own effort; we have received it from Him as
a gift. Sin caused an estrangement; the cross has accomplished an atonement. Sin bred enmity; the cross has
brought peace. Sin created a gulf between man and
God; the cross has bridged it. Sin broke the fellowship;
the cross has restored it. To state the same truth in
different words, as St. Paul did to the Romans, 'the
wages of sin is death, but the free gift of God is eternal
life in Christ Jesus our Lord' (Rom. vi. 23).

In seeking now to convey what the Bible teaches
concerning the cross, two matters will receive emphasis,
first the centrality of the cross, and secondly its meaning.

I. THE CENTRALITY OF THE CROSS

It is not an exaggeration to say that the central figure
of the Bible is Jesus Christ, and that the central feature
of His career as it is there portrayed is His death. Nor
is this surprising, for the purpose of the Bible is
essentially practical. It is a handbook of salvation for
sinners. If this is so, it is inevitable that Christ crucified
will be prominent, for it is in Him that salvation is to

be found. Thus the risen Jesus was able to rebuke the
two disciples whom He had accompanied on their walk
to Emmaus. They possessed the Scriptures and had read
them, but had failed to detect the necessity of His death!
'O foolish men', He cried, 'and slow of heart to believe
all that the prophets have spoken! Was it not necessary
that the Christ should suffer these things and enter into
his glory?' And St. Luke adds that 'beginning with
Moses and all the prophets, he interpreted to them in all
the scriptures the things concerning himself' (Lk. xxiv.
25-27).

The religion of the Old Testament was sacrificial
from the beginning. Ever since Abel 'brought of the
firstlings of his flock and of their fat portions. And the
Lord had regard for Abel and his offering' (Gn. iv.
4, 5), worshippers of Jehovah brought sacrifices to Him.
Altars were built, animals were killed and blood was
shed long before the levitical laws of Moses. But under
Moses, after the covenant had been ratified between
God and the people at Mount Sinai, what had been
spontaneous and haphazard was regularized by divine
ordinance. The great prophets of the eighth and
seventh centuries BC protested against the formalism and
immorality of the worshippers, but the sacrificial system
continued without interruption until the destruction of
the Temple in AD 70. Every Jew was familiar with the
ritual attached to burnt offering, meal offering, thank
offering, sin offering, trespass offering and their
appropriate drink offerings, as well as with the special
occasions, daily, weekly, monthly and yearly when they
had to be offered. No Jew, be he never so obtuse, could
have failed to learn the fundamental lesson of all this
educative process that 'without the shedding of blood
there is no forgiveness of sins' (Heb. ix. 22).

If the sacrifices of the Old Testament in some measure
visibly prefigured the greater sacrifice of Christ, the
prophets and psalmists predicted His sufferings too. We
can see Him dimly foreshadowed in the character of
the innocent sufferer who is unjustly persecuted in
various psalms, which were later applied to Jesus. We
detect Him in Zechariah's shepherd who is smitten and

whose sheep are scattered abroad (xiii. 7; cf. Mk. xiv. 27), and in Daniel's prince or 'anointed one' who is 'cut off' (ix. 25, 26). Above all, we can find Him in the noble figure who appears in the Servant Songs towards the end of the Book of Isaiah, the suffering servant of Jehovah, the despised 'man of sorrows', who is wounded for the transgressions of others, bruised for their inquities, goes like a lamb to the slaughter and bears the sins of many (chapter liii). Truly, 'thus it is written, that the Christ should suffer' (Lk. xxiv. 46).

When Jesus came, He knew Himself to be a son of destiny. He recognized that the Scriptures were bearing witness to Him and that it was in Him that their great expectation was to be fulfilled. This is particularly clear in reference to His coming sufferings. The turning point of His ministry came at Caesarea Philippi when, immediately after Simon Peter had confessed Him to be the Christ, 'he began to teach them that the Son of man must suffer many things' (Mk. viii. 31). It is this 'must', this sense of compulsion laid upon Him by the Scriptures as revealing the Father's will, which continually recurs in His teaching. He knew He had 'a baptism to be baptized with' and felt Himself constrained until it was accomplished (Lk. xii. 50). He kept moving steadily towards His 'hour', which in St. John's Gospel is said several times not to have come, and of which at last, shortly before His arrest, with the cross in sight, He could say, 'Father, the hour has come' (Jn. xvii. 1). The prospect of the ordeal before Him filled Him with aweful foreboding. 'Now is my soul troubled', He cried out. 'And what shall I say, "Father, save me from this hour"? No, for this purpose I have come to this hour. Father, glorify thy name' (Jn. xii. 27, 28). When at last the moment of His arrest arrived, and Simon lunged out with his sword to protect Him, slashing the ear of the high priest's servant, Jesus rebuked him, 'Put your sword into its sheath; shall I not drink the cup which the Father has given me?' (Jn. xviii. 11). According to Matthew, Jesus added, 'Do you think that I cannot appeal to my Father, and he will at once send me more than twelve legions of angels? But how then should the scriptures be fulfilled, that it must be so?' (Mt. xxvi. 53, 54).

The supreme importance of the cross which the Old Testament foretold and Jesus taught is fully recognized by the New Testament authors. The evangelists devote a disproportionate amount of space to Christ's last week and death, in comparison to His life and ministry. Two-fifths of the first Gospel, three-fifths of the second, one-third of the third, and almost one-half of the fourth, are allotted to an account of the events between His triumphal entry into Jerusalem and His triumphant ascension into heaven. It is particularly striking in the case of St. John, whose Gospel has sometimes been divided into two equal halves which have been entitled 'The Book of the Signs' and 'The Book of the Passion'.

What is implied in the Gospels is stated explicitly in the Epistles, and most notably by St. Paul. The apostle never grew tired of reminding his readers of the cross. He had himself a vivid sense of indebtedness to the Saviour who had died for him. 'The Son of God . . . loved me', he could write, 'and gave himself for me' (Gal. ii. 20), and therefore, 'God forbid that I should glory, save in the cross of our Lord Jesus Christ' (Gal. vi. 14 AV). This experience and this resolve were clearly reflected in his ministry. The priority which he gave to the message of the cross in his preaching is nowhere made more plain than in his first letter to the Corinthians. They were in danger of being entangled in the subtleties of Greek philosophy, but the apostle would not compromise the gospel. Let the 'Jews demand signs', he wrote, and let the 'Greeks seek wisdom, but we preach Christ crucified, a stumbling-block to Jews and folly to Gentiles, but to those who are called, both Jews and Greeks, Christ the power of God and the wisdom of God' (i. 22-24). This was what Paul had in fact proclaimed when he first came to Corinth from Athens in his second missionary journey, 'I decided to know nothing among you except Jesus Christ and him crucified' (ii. 2), and again (xv. 3), 'I delivered to you as of first importance what I also received, that Christ died for our sins in accordance with the scriptures.'

What St. Peter thought and wrote of the cross we shall see later, in the Epistle to the Hebrews it is declared unequivocally that Christ 'has appeared once for all at the end of the age to put away sin by the sacrifice of himself' (ix. 26), and when we reach the mysterious and wonderful Book of the Revelation, we catch a glimpse of the glorified Jesus by the throne of God in heaven not only as 'the Lion of the tribe of Judah' but as 'a Lamb standing, as though it had been slain' (v. 5, 6), and we hear the countless multitude of saints and angels singing His praise, 'Worthy is the Lamb who was slain, to receive power and wealth and wisdom and might and honour and glory and blessing!' (v. 12).

So from the early chapters of Genesis to the final chapters of the Revelation we can trace what some writers have called a scarlet thread. It is in fact like the thread of Theseus which enables us to find our way through the labyrinth of Scripture. And what the Bible teaches concerning the centrality of the cross of our Saviour, the Christian Church has recognized. Many churches mark us with the sign of a cross at our baptism and erect a cross over our grave when we are dead. Churches have often been built in a cruciform shape, and many Christians wear a cross on lapel, necklace or chain. None of this is accidental. The cross is the symbol of our faith. What the Emperor Constantine is said to have seen in the sky, we can see ourselves in the pages of the Bible. *'In hoc signo vinces.'* There is no conquest without the cross. There is no Christianity without the cross.

II. THE MEANING OF THE CROSS

Having attempted to establish the centrality of the cross, I must now seek to unfold its meaning. Yet I cannot begin the task without frankly confessing that much remains a mystery. The cross is the pivotal event in history. Small wonder that our puny minds cannot fully take it in! One day the veil will be altogether removed, and all riddles will be solved. We shall see Christ as He is and worship Him through eternity for what He has done. 'Now we see in a mirror dimly, but then face to face. Now I know in part; then I shall understand fully, even as I have been fully understood' (1 Cor. xiii. 12). So said the great apostle Paul with his massive intellect and his many revelations; and if he said it, how much more should we?

I shall content myself, then, with an endeavour to explain some references to the death of Jesus made by Simon Peter in his first Epistle. I turn to the writings of Peter on purpose. I have three reasons.

First, because Peter was one of the inner and intimate three. 'Peter, James and John' form a trio who enjoyed a closer fellowship with Jesus than the rest of the Twelve. Peter is therefore as likely as anyone to have grasped what Jesus thought and taught concerning His death. Indeed, we find in his first Epistle several clear reminiscences of his Master's teaching.

Second, I turn to Peter with confidence, because he was himself at first very reluctant to accept the necessity of Christ's sufferings. He had been the first to acknowledge Christ's person, but he was the first to deny the need for His death. He who had declared, 'Thou art the Christ' shouted vehemently, 'No, Lord' when Jesus began to teach that the Christ must suffer. Throughout the remaining days of Christ's ministry, Peter retained his dogged hostility to the idea of a Christ who would die. He tried to defend Him in the garden, and, when the arrest was a *fait accompli*, followed Him afar off. In sullen disillusionment he denied Him three times in the courtyard, and the tears he wept were not only of remorse but of despair. Only after the resurrection, when Jesus taught the apostles from the Scriptures that it was 'necessary that the Christ should suffer these things and enter into his glory' (Lk. xxiv. 26), did Simon Peter at last begin to understand and believe. Within a few weeks he had laid hold of the truth so firmly that he could address the crowd in the Temple cloisters with the words, 'what God foretold by the mouth of all the prophets, that his Christ should suffer, he thus fulfilled' (Acts iii. 18), and his first Epistle contains several references to 'the sufferings and glory of the Christ'. We too may at first be reluctant to admit the necessity, and slow to fathom the meaning, of the cross, but if anyone can persuade us and teach us, it will be Simon Peter.

Third, the references to the cross in St. Peter's first Epistle are asides. If Peter had set himself deliberately to argue the indispensability of Christ's passion, we might have suspected him of being tendentious and therefore unreliable. But his references are artless and guileless. He is not elaborating subtle theological doctrines; he is enforcing plain ethical duties. He urges them to be holy and to bear suffering patiently, and then refers them to the cross for their inspiration and example.

The longest section in the Epistle which relates to the death of Christ is in the second chapter and runs from verse 18 to the end of the chapter. I propose that we examine it in some detail. We shall find Peter indicating that the crucified Jesus died firstly as an example, and secondly as a 'sinbearer'.

a. Christ died as our Example

Persecution is the background to this Epistle. The Emperor Nero was known to be hostile to the Christian Church, and the hearts of many Christians were failing them for fear. Already spasmodic outbreaks of violence had occurred. It seemed that worse was to come. The case of Christian slaves in the household of a pagan master was particularly problematical. Supposing they were ill-treated? How should they behave? It was partly to answer these questions that Peter wrote his letter to Christians scattered in the Roman provinces of Pontus, Galatia, Cappadocia, Asia and Bithynia. The advice he gives is straightforward. Let them be sure that they are not receiving punishment which they deserve. It is no credit to them to accept a beating for wrongdoing. Let them rather suffer for righteousness' sake and welcome reproach for the name of Christ. They are not to resist, still less to retaliate. They must submit. To bear unjust suffering patiently has God's approval. Then at once Peter's mind flies to the cross. Undeserved suffering is part of the Christian's calling, he asserts, 'because Christ also suffered for you, leaving you an example, that you should follow in his steps' (ii. 21). He was sinless and guileless. Yet when He was insulted, He took no revenge; when He suffered, He uttered no threats. He simply committed Himself, or as the text may rather read, He committed them (His tormentors), into the hands of the just Judge of men.

He has left us an example. The Greek word Peter uses, unique here in the New Testament, denotes a teacher's copybook, the perfect alphabet on which a pupil models his script as he learns to write. If we would master the ABC of Christian love, we must trace out our lives according to the pattern of Jesus. We must 'follow in His steps'. The word is eloquent as it comes from Peter's pen. He had boasted that he would follow Jesus to prison and to death, but in the event had 'followed afar off'. Only on the shore of Galilee had Jesus renewed His call and commission to Peter in His familiar terms 'Follow me' (Jn. xxi. 19, 22). So Peter was urging his readers to join him as he tried to follow now more obediently in the Master's steps.

The challenge of the cross is as uncomfortable in the twentieth century as it was in the first, and is as relevant to ordinary citizens in their homes and jobs today as ever it was to slaves in Roman households. Perhaps nothing is more absolutely opposed to our natural instincts than this command to submit and to forbear resistance, to bear unjust suffering, and to overcome evil with good. We so quickly rush to our own defence. We are knocked down, and immediately like a jack-in-a-box we are up again and ready to give as good as we got. But the cross bids us accept the injury, love the enemy and entrust the issue to God.

But the death of Jesus is not only an inspiring example. If it were nothing more, much in the Gospel narratives would be inexplicable. What is the meaning of those sayings of Jesus in which He declared that the Son of man had come 'not to be served but to serve, and to give his life as a ransom for many' (Mk. x. 45), and again in the upper room that the wine was His 'blood of the covenant, which is poured out for many for the forgiveness of sins' (Mt. xxvi. 28)? If His death was a ransom price by which captives are set free, and if the shedding of His blood ratified a new covenant between God and man whose terms included the forgiveness of sins, then it was not just a moral spectacle to be admired and copied. There is no redemption in an example. A pattern cannot secure our pardon. Besides, why was His soul burdened with such heavy and anxious foreboding as the cross approached? and how shall we explain the dreadful agony in the garden, His tears and cries and bloody sweat? 'My Father, if it be possible, let this cup pass from me; nevertheless, not as I will, but as thou wilt.' 'My Father, if this cannot pass unless I drink it, thy will be done' (Mt. xxvi. 39, 42). Was the cup from which He shrank the symbol of death by crucifixion? Was He then afraid of pain and death? If so, His example may have been one of submission and patience, but it was hardly one of courage. Socrates, Plato tells us, drank his cup of hemlock in his prison cell in Athens 'quite readily and cheerfully'. Was Socrates braver than Jesus?—or were their cups filled with different poison? and what is the meaning of the darkness, and the cry of dereliction, and the rending of the Temple veil from top to bottom? These things have no meaning if Jesus died only as an example. Indeed some of them seem to make His example less exemplary.

Not only would much in the Gospels remain mysterious if Christ's death were purely an example, but our human need would remain unsatisfied. We do not simply need an example; we need a Saviour. An example can stir our imagination, kindle our idealism and strengthen our resolve, but it cannot cleanse the defilement of our past sins, bring peace to our troubled conscience or fetch us home to God.

In any case, the apostles leave us in no doubt about the matter. They regularly associate Christ's coming and death with our sins. 'Christ died for our sins in accordance with the scriptures' (1 Cor. xv. 3); 'Christ also died for sins once for all' (1 Pet. iii. 18). 'You know that he appeared to take away sins' (1 Jn. iii. 5). Here are the three great apostolic writers of the New Testament, St.

Paul, St. Peter and St. John, unanimous in linking His death with our sins.

b. Christ died as our Sinbearer

The phrase which Peter uses here in ii. 24 is 'he himself bore our sins in his body on the tree'. The expression to 'bear sin' has a rather foreign sound in our ears, and we shall need to go back to the Old Testament to understand it. The idea occurs most frequently in the books of Leviticus and Numbers. Many times it is written of an offender who infringes one of God's revealed laws that 'he shall bear his iniquity' or 'he shall bear his sin'. For instance, in a passage dealing with the duties of priests and Levites after the rebellion of Korah, it is written, 'And henceforth the people of Israel shall not come near the tent of meeting, lest they bear sin and die.' Again, 'If any one sins, doing any of the things which the Lord has commanded not to be done . . . he is guilty and shall bear his iniquity' (Nu. xviii. 22; Lv. v. 17).

But sometimes it is implied that somebody else can assume responsibility for the sinner. In the thirtieth chapter of the book Numbers, which deals with the validity of vows, Moses explains that a vow taken by a man or a widow must stand. A vow, however, taken by an unmarried girl, or a married woman, must be validated by her father and her husband respectively. If on the day on which the man hears of the woman's vow, he does not invalidate it, and it later proves to be foolish, it is said, 'he shall bear her iniquity' (Nu. xxx. 15).

This possibility of somebody else accepting the responsibility for, and bearing the consequences of, our sins, was further taught by those Old Testament blood sacrifices in the Mosaic legislation which seem so strange to us today. Of the sin offering it was stated, 'God hath given it you to bear the iniquity of the congregation, to make atonement for them before the Lord' (Lv. x. 17 AV). Similarly, on the annual Day of Atonement, Aaron was instructed to lay his hands on the head of the scapegoat, thus identifying himself and his people with it; he was then to confess the nation's sins, symbolically transferring them to the goat, which was driven out into the wilderness; and next we read, 'The goat shall bear all their iniquities upon him to a solitary land' (Lv. xvi. 22). This makes it plain that 'to bear sin' means to bear the penalty for sin.

Despite this amazing temporary provision, 'it is impossible that the blood of bulls and goats should take away sins' (Heb. x. 4). So in the longest Servant Song of Isaiah (chapter liii), the innocent sufferer (who foreshadows Christ) is described in terms which are intentionally sacrificial. He was 'like a lamb that is led to the slaughter' not only because 'he opened not his mouth' but also because 'the Lord has laid on him the iniquity of us all', and His soul was made 'an offering for sin'. We all 'like sheep have gone astray', but He also 'like a sheep' 'was wounded for our transgressions, he was bruised for our iniquities; upon him was the chastisement that made us whole, and with his stripes we are healed'. Now all this clear language of substitution, describing Him as 'stricken for the transgression of my people', is summed up in the chapter in the two phrases with which we have been made familiar by Leviticus, 'he shall bear their iniquities' and 'he bore the sin of many'.

At last Jesus arrived, heralded by the law and the prophets, and John the Baptist publicly hailed Him, 'Behold, the Lamb of God, who takes away the sin of the world!', and again the next day, more simply, 'Behold, the Lamb of God!' (Jn. i. 29, 36). The New Testament authors have no difficulty in recognizing His death as the sacrifice in which all the Levitical sacrifices reach their final fulfilment, and this truth forms part of the message of the Epistle to the Hebrews. The old sacrifices were of bulls and goats; Christ offered Himself. The old sacrifices were interminably repeated; Christ died once and for all. He was 'offered once to bear the sins of many' (Heb. ix. 28). This last phrase brings us back to St. Peter's expression, 'he himself bore our sins in his body on the tree' (1 Pet. ii. 24). The Son of God identified Himself with the sins of men. He was not

content to take our nature upon Him; He took our
iniquity upon Him as well. He was not only 'made flesh'
in the womb of Mary; He was 'made sin' on the cross
of Calvary. These last words are St. Paul's (2 Cor. v. 21)
and are among the most startling in the whole biblical
teaching about the atonement. But we cannot escape
their significance. In the previous verses Paul has
affirmed that God refused to impute our sins to us, or
count them against us (2 Cor. v. 19). That is, in His
utterly undeserved love to us, He would not hold us
responsible for our sins. He would not have it said of us
as it was of so many in Old Testament days, 'they shall
bear their iniquity.' Then what did He do? 'For our
sake he made him to be sin who knew no sin, so that
in him we might become the righteousness of God' (v.
21). Christ had no sins of His own; He was made sin
with our sins, on the cross.

As we look at the cross, we can begin to understand
the terrible implications of these words. At twelve noon
'there was darkness over the whole land' (Mk. xv. 33)
which continued for three hours until He died. With
the darkness came silence, for no eye should see, and no
lips could tell, the agony of soul which the spotless Lamb
of God endured. The accumulated sins of the whole
world and of all history were laid upon Him. Voluntarily
He bore them in His own body. He made them His own.
He shouldered full responsibility for them. And then in
desolate spiritual abandonment that woeful cry was
wrung from His lips, 'My God, my God, why hast thou
forsaken me?' (Mk. xv. 34). It was a quotation from the
first verse of Psalm xxii. Perhaps He had been meditat-
ing during His agony on its description of the sufferings
and glory of the Christ. But why did He quote that
verse? Why not one of the triumphant verses at the
end? Why not, 'You who fear the Lord, praise him!'
(verse 23) or 'Dominion belongs to the Lord' (verse 28)?
Are we to believe that it was a cry of human weakness
or despair, or that the Son of God was imagining things?
It is far better to adopt the traditional view and to take
these words at their face value. He was bearing our
sins. And God who is 'of purer eyes than to behold evil'

and cannot 'look on wrong' (Hab. i. 13) hid His face.
Our sins came between the Father and the Son. The
Lord Jesus who lived eternally in the bosom of the
Father and enjoyed unbroken communion with the
Father throughout the days of His flesh, was thus
momentarily abandoned. In a word, our sins sent Christ
to hell. He tasted the torment of a soul estranged from
God. Bearing our sins, He died our death, and so
endured instead of us the penalty of separation from
God which our sins deserved. He 'gave himself as a
ransom for all' (1 Tim. ii. 6).

At once, emerging from that outer darkness, He cried
in triumph, 'It is finished', and then, 'Father, into thy
hands I commit my spirit', and He died (Jn. xix. 30;
Lk. xxiii. 46). The work He had come to do was finished.
The salvation He had come to win was accomplished.
The sins of the world were borne. Reconciliation to God
was available to all who would trust this Saviour for
themselves, and receive Him as their own. So, as if to
give a public witness to this fact, the unseen hand of
God tore down the veil of the Temple and hurled it
aside. It was needed no longer. The way into God's holy
presence was no longer barred. Christ had 'opened the
gate of heaven to all believers'.

This simple and wonderful tale of the sinbearing of
the Son of God is strangely unpopular today. That He
should have borne our sins and taken our penalty is said
to be immoral or unworthy or unjust. And of course it
can easily be travestied. We are not suggesting that there
is nothing left for us to do. Of course we must return
'to the Shepherd and Guardian of our souls', dying to sin
and living to righteousness (1 Pet. ii. 25, 24). Above all
we do not forget that 'all this is from God', issuing from
His unimaginable mercy. He did not inflict a penalty
on Christ which He was not willing to bear Himself.
'God was in Christ reconciling the world unto himself.'
How He can have been in Christ while He made Christ
to be sin for us, I cannot explain, but the same apostle
states these two truths in the same paragraph. And I
accept the paradox as I do the equally baffling paradox
that Jesus of Nazareth was both Man and God, and yet

one person. If there was a paradox in His person, it is not surprising that we find one in His work also.

But even if we cannot resolve the paradox or fathom the mystery, we should accept the direct statement of Christ and His apostles, that He bore our sins, understanding the phrase in its biblical meaning that He underwent the penalty of our sins for us. That St. Peter meant this is clear from three considerations. First, he says that it was on the 'tree' that Christ bore our sins. No doubt the word was used deliberately, just as he used it in his early sermons as they are recorded in the Acts, e.g., 'The God of our fathers raised Jesus whom you killed by hanging him on a tree' (Acts v. 30). The Jewish Sanhedrin would clearly have understood the implied reference to Deuteronomy xxi. 23, where it was written, 'Cursed is every man that hangeth on a tree' (AV). The fact that Jesus ended His life hanging on a 'tree' (for the Jews regarded nailing to a cross and hanging on a tree as equivalents) meant that He was under the divine curse. Instead of repudiating this idea, the apostles accepted it, and St. Paul explained it in Galatians iii. 'Cursed be every one who does not abide by all things written in the book of the law, and do them' (verse 10). But 'Christ redeemed us from the curse of the law, having become a curse for us—for it is written, "Cursed be every one who hangs on a tree"' (verse 13). The plain meaning of these verses in the context is that the curse resting on transgressors was transferred to Jesus on the cross. He has freed us from the curse by taking it upon Himself when He died.

Second, this passage in Peter's first Epistle contains no fewer than five clear verbal reminiscences of Isaiah liii. It may be helpful to tabulate them.

1 Peter ii	Isaiah liii
Verse 22	*Verse 9*
He committed no sin; no guile was found on his lips	He had done no violence, and there was no deceit in his mouth
Verse 23	*Verse 3*
He was reviled	He was despised and rejected by men

E

1 Peter ii	Isaiah liii
Verse 24 He himself bore our sins	*Verse 12* He bore the sin of many
Verse 24 By his wounds you have been healed	*Verse 5* With his stripes we are healed
Verse 25 You were straying like sheep	*Verse 6* All we like sheep have gone astray

We have already seen that the fifty-third chapter of Isaiah portrays an innocent sufferer who in a sacrificial death is wounded for the transgressions of others. There is no doubt that Jesus Himself interpreted His mission and death in the light of this chapter, as did His disciples after Him. When the Ethiopian eunuch asked the evangelist Philip to whom the prophet was referring in this chapter that he was reading in his chariot, Philip immediately 'told him the good news of Jesus' (Acts viii. 35).

Third, Peter has other references to the cross in his Epistle which confirm our interpretation of his words in the second chapter. In the first chapter he describes his readers as having been 'ransomed . . . with the precious blood of Christ, like that of a lamb without blemish or spot' (verses 18, 19), while in the second verse of the Epistle he speaks of being sprinkled with Christ's blood. Now these two phrases refer to the original Passover sacrifice at the time of the Exodus. Each Israelite family took a lamb, killed it, and sprinkled its blood on the lintel and side posts of the house. Only so were they safe from the judgment of God and only so did they escape from the slavery of Egypt. Peter boldly applies the Passover to Christ (as does Paul also, 'Christ, our paschal lamb, has been sacrificed', 1 Cor. v. 7). His blood was shed to redeem us from the judgment of God and the bondage of sin. It must be sprinkled on our hearts. Peter's other significant reference to the cross is in iii. 18: 'Christ also died for sins once for all, the righteous for the unrighteous, that he might bring us to God. . . . ' Sin has separated us from God; but Christ desired to bring us back to God. So He suffered for our sins, an innocent Saviour dying for guilty sinners, and He did it once for all. He 'made there (by His one oblation of Himself once offered) a full, perfect, and sufficient sacrifice, oblation, and satisfaction, for the sins of the whole world'.[1] What He has done can therefore be neither improved, nor repeated. No religious observances or righteous works of ours can earn our forgiveness. Indeed, to seek to secure God's favour by our own efforts is an insult to Jesus Christ. It is to insinuate that His sacrifice was not necessary, and that He need not have bothered to die. 'If justification (i.e. acceptance before God) were through the law, then Christ died to no purpose' (Gal. ii. 21). If we could accomplish our own salvation, the atonement of Christ was redundant.

The message of the cross remains, in our day as in St. Paul's, a stumbling-block to some and folly to others; but it has brought peace to the conscience of millions. As Richard Hooker wrote in a sermon which he preached in 1585 when he was Master of the Temple, 'Let it be accounted folly, or frenzy, or fury, or whatsoever. It is our wisdom and our comfort; we care for no knowledge in the world but this, that man hath sinned and God hath suffered; that God hath made Himself the sin of men, and that men are made the righteousness of God.' Every Christian can echo these words. There is healing through His wounds, life through His death, pardon through His pain, salvation through His suffering.

Almighty God, who hast given Thine only Son to be unto us both a sacrifice for sin, and also an ensample of godly life. Give us grace that we may always most thankfully receive that His inestimable benefit, and also daily endeavour ourselves to follow the blessed steps of His most holy life; through the same Jesus Christ our Lord.[2] Amen.

---

[1] *Book of Common Prayer,* from the Prayer of Consecration in the Service of Holy Communion.
[2] Collect for the second Sunday after Easter.

CHAPTER VIII

THE SPIRIT OF CHRIST AND THE CHURCH OF CHRIST

IT is a great mistake to suppose that the salvation of Christ means merely the settlement of our past sins. He is as much concerned with the present and future as with the past. If He can secure our forgiveness and our reconciliation to God, He can overcome the other evil consequences of sin as well. Salvation is a comprehensive term. It embraces not only our acceptance with God, but our progressive liberation from the tyranny of selfishness and the restoration of harmonious relations with our fellow men. The first of these blessings we owe chiefly to the death of Christ, but it is by His Spirit that we can be set free from ourselves and by His Church that we can be united in a fellowship of love. It is to these aspects of Christ's salvation that we give attention in this chapter.

I. THE SPIRIT OF CHRIST

We have already seen that our sins should be viewed not just as a series of unrelated incidents, but as the symptoms of an inward moral disease. Jesus several times used the simile of the tree and the fruit. The quality of fruits, He taught, depends on the quality of the tree which bears them. 'Every sound tree bears good fruit, but the bad tree bears evil fruit. A sound tree cannot bear evil fruit, nor can a bad tree bear good fruit' (Mt. vii. 17, 18). The cause of our sins, therefore, is our sin, our inherited nature which is perverted and self-centred. Jesus called this nature the 'heart' of man, and stated: 'From within, out of the heart of man, come evil thoughts, fornication, theft, murder, adultery, coveting, wickedness, deceit, licentiousness, envy, slander, pride, foolishness. All these evil things come from within, and they defile a man.' Similarly, 'out of the abundance of the heart the mouth speaks . . . the evil man out of his evil treasure brings forth evil' (Mk. vii. 21-23; Mt. xii. 34, 35).

Our outward behaviour is thus seen to be the expression of our inward nature. It stands to reason that an improvement in behaviour depends on a change of nature. 'Make the tree good', said Jesus, 'and its fruit (will be) good' (Mt. xii. 33). But can human nature be changed? Is it possible to make a sour person sweet, a proud person humble, or a selfish person unselfish? The Bible declares emphatically that these miracles can take place. This is part of the glory of the gospel. Jesus Christ offers to change not only our standing before God but our very nature. He spoke of the indispensable necessity of a new birth. His disturbing words to Nicodemus are still applicable to us: 'Truly, truly, I say to you, unless one is born anew, he cannot see the kingdom of God. . . . Do not marvel that I said to you, "You must be born anew" ' (Jn. iii. 3, 7). St. Paul's words are in some ways even more dramatic when he blurts out, in a sentence which has no verbs : 'If any man in Christ—new creation!' (2 Cor. v. 17, literally). Here then is the possibility of which the New Testament speaks—a new heart, a new nature, a new birth, a new creation. The spring can be so cleansed that the stream becomes pure.

This tremendous inward change is the work of the Holy Spirit. The new birth is a birth 'from above'. To be born again is to be 'born of the Spirit' (Jn. iii. 6). It is hardly relevant here to discuss the mysterious doctrine of the Trinity. For our present purpose it is sufficient to consider what the early apostles wrote about the Holy Spirit, as their teaching was illumined by their own experience.

First, however, it is important to realize that the Holy Spirit neither came into existence, nor began to be active, at Pentecost. He is God. He is therefore eternal and has been at work in the world since the creation. The Old Testament has many references to Him, and the prophets looked forward to the Christian dispensation as a time when His activity would increase and spread. Ezekiel and Jeremiah in particular spoke of His future work within God's people. 'A new heart I will give you, and a new spirit I will put within you; and I will take out of your flesh the heart of stone and give you a heart of flesh. And I will put my spirit within you, and cause you to walk in my statutes and be careful to observe my ordinances.' Here the gift of a new heart is closely linked with the indwelling of God's Spirit, and the result will be a life of obedience to His law. Jeremiah's wonderful prophecy of the new covenant includes a similar provision, 'I will put my law within them, and I will write it upon their hearts' (Ezk. xxxvi. 26, 27; Je. xxxi. 33). The people of God will no longer have an external code engraved on stone tablets which they cannot obey, but the law of God written in their hearts by the Holy Spirit, who will not only teach it to them but give them power to conform their lives to its requirements.

What the Old Testament prophets foretold about seven hundred years before Christ, Christ promised as an immediate expectation. A few hours before He died, secluded in the upper room with the Twelve, He spoke of 'the Comforter', 'the Spirit of truth', who would come and take His place. Indeed, the Holy Spirit's presence would be better for them even than His own earthly presence had been. 'It is to your advantage that I go away,' He said, 'for if I do not go away, the Counsellor will not come to you; but if I go, I will send him to you.' The advantage was simply this. Christ had only been *with* them, at their side; but 'he . . . will be *in* you' (Jn. xvi. 7, xiv. 17). There is a sense in which we may reverently say that the teaching ministry of Jesus had proved a failure. Several times He had put a child in the midst and urged the disciples to humble themselves, but Simon Peter remained proud and self-confident. Often He taught them to love one another, but even John seems to have deserved his nickname 'son of thunder' to the end. Yet when you read Peter's first Epistle you cannot fail to notice its references to humility, and John's Epistles are full of love. What made the difference? The Holy Spirit. Jesus taught them to be humble and loving; but they did not exhibit either quality until the Holy Spirit entered their personality and began to change them from within.

On the Day of Pentecost 'they were all filled with the Holy Spirit'. Do not imagine that this was a freak experience for apostles and other eminent saints. 'Be filled with the Spirit' is a command addressed to all Christians. The inner presence of the Holy Spirit is the spiritual birthright of every Christian. Indeed, if the Holy Spirit has not taken up residence within us, we are not real Christians at all. 'Any one who does not have the Spirit of Christ does not belong to him,' Paul wrote (see Acts ii. 4; Eph. v. 18; Rom. viii. 9).

This then is what the New Testament teaches. When we put our trust in Jesus Christ and commit ourselves to Him, the Holy Spirit enters us. He is sent by God 'into our hearts'. He makes our bodies His temple (Gal. iv. 6; 1 Cor. vi. 19).

This does not mean that from now on we are exempt from the possibility of sinning. On the contrary, in some ways the conflict is intensified; but, on the other hand, a way of victory has been opened. St. Paul gives a vivid description of the battle in the fifth chapter of his letter to the Galatians. The combatants are 'the flesh', his name for our inherited self-centred nature, and 'the Spirit'. 'The desires of the flesh', he explains, 'are against the Spirit, and the desires of the Spirit are against the flesh; for these are opposed to each other . . . ' (Gal. v. 17). This is not arid theological theorizing; this is the daily experience of every Christian. We continue to feel sinful desires which are tugging us down; but we are now also conscious of a counteracting force pulling us upwards to holiness. If 'the flesh' were given free rein, it would stampede us into the dark jungle of immoral and selfish vices which Paul lists in verses 19 to 21. If, on the other hand, the Holy Spirit is allowed His way, the result will be 'love, joy, peace, patience, kindness, goodness, faithfulness, gentleness, self-control' (Gal. v. 22, 23). These attractive virtues are called by St. Paul 'the fruit of the Spirit' (Gal. v. 22, 23). The human character is likened to an orchard which the Holy Spirit is cultivating. Let Him make the trees good, and their fruit will be good also.

How then can 'the flesh' be overcome, with its hideous works, so that 'the fruit of the Spirit' may grow and ripen? The answer lies in the inner attitude which we adopt towards each. 'Those who belong to Christ Jesus have crucified the flesh with its passions and desires.' 'Walk by (or, in) the Spirit, and do not (or you will not) gratify the desires of the flesh' (Gal. v. 24, 16). Towards 'the flesh' we must take up such an attitude of fierce resistance and ruthless rejection that only the word 'crucifixion' can describe it; but to the indwelling Spirit we must trustfully surrender the undisputed dominion over our lives. The more we make a habit of denying the flesh and yielding to the Spirit, the more the ugly works of the flesh will disappear and the lovely fruit of the Spirit will take their place.

St. Paul teaches the same truth in 2 Corinthians iii. 18: 'We all, with unveiled face, beholding the glory of the Lord, are being changed into his likeness from one degree of glory to another; for this comes from the Lord who is the Spirit.' It is by the Spirit of Christ that we can be transformed into the image of Christ, as we keep looking steadfastly towards Him. We thus have our part to play, in repentance and faith and discipline, but essentially holiness is the work of the Holy Spirit.

> And every virtue we possess,
>   And every victory won,
> And every thought of holiness,
>   Are His alone.
>
> Spirit of purity and grace,
>   Our weakness, pitying, see;
> O make our hearts Thy dwelling-place,
>   And worthier Thee!

Archbishop William Temple used to illustrate this lesson in this way: 'It is no good giving me a play like Hamlet or King Lear, and telling me to write a play like that. Shakespeare could do it; I can't. And it is no good showing me a life like the life of Jesus and telling me to live a life like that. Jesus could do it; I can't. But if the genius of Shakespeare could come and live in me, then I could write plays like that. And if the Spirit of Jesus could come and live in me, then I could live a life like that.' This is the secret of Christian sanctity. It is not just that we should strive to live like Jesus, but that Jesus by His Spirit should come and live in us. To have Him as our example is not enough; we need Him as our Saviour. It is thus through His atoning death that the penalty of our sins may be forgiven; whereas it is through His indwelling Spirit that the power of our sins may be broken.

II. THE CHURCH OF CHRIST

Sin manifests a centrifugal tendency. It pulls people out of harmony with their neighbours. It estranges them not only from their Maker but from their fellow-creatures. We all know from experience how a community, whether a school, a hospital, a factory or an office, can become a hotbed of rivalries and suspicions. We find it very difficult 'to dwell together in unity'.

God's purpose has been to overthrow through Christ all the vile consequences of sin. His plan, therefore, is not to call independent, unconnected individuals to return to Himself in isolation from one another, but to redeem a people for His own possession.

Already in the early chapters of Genesis this is made clear. God called Abraham to leave his home and kindred in Mesopotamia, and promised to give him not only a land for his inheritance but a seed as numerous as the stars in the sky and the sand on the seashore. This pledge to multiply the descendants of Abraham and through them to bless all the nations of the earth was renewed to his son Isaac and his grandson Jacob.

Jacob, however, died in exile in Egypt, whither he and his sons had gone when famine overtook the land of Canaan. His twelve sons survived him and became the fathers of the twelve tribes of 'Israel', the name God had given to Jacob. With these 'children of Israel', rescued years later from their Egyptian slavery, God renewed His covenant.

But how were all the families of the earth to be blessed? Century followed century, as the fortunes of Israel unfolded, and still the nation seemed to the rest of the world more a curse than a blessing. Surrounded by high walls of their own building, God's people protected themselves from defiling contact with the unclean Gentiles. It seemed as if they would miss their destiny as benefactors of the world. Was God's promise to Abraham to prove a lie? No. Many of the prophets knew by the word of the Lord that when the Messiah came, God's own anointed Prince, pilgrims would come from every point of the compass to enter the kingdom of God.

At last the Christ came. Jesus of Nazareth announced the arrival of the long-awaited kingdom. Many would come, He said, from north, south, east and west, and sit down with Abraham, Isaac and Jacob. God's people would no longer be a race apart, but a society whose members were drawn from every nation, kindred and tongue. 'Go . . . ', the risen Lord commanded His followers, 'and make disciples of all nations . . . ' (Mt. xxviii. 19). The sum total of these disciples He called 'my church' (Mt. xvi. 18).

So God's pledge to Abraham, repeated several times to him and renewed to his sons, is being fulfilled in the growth of the world-wide Church today. 'If you are Christ's,' wrote St. Paul, 'then you are Abraham's offspring, heirs according to promise' (Gal. iii. 29).

One of the most striking pictures which the apostle uses to convey the unity of believers in Christ is that of the human body. The Church, he says, is the body of Christ. Every Christian is a member or organ of the body, while Christ Himself is the Head, controlling the body's activities. Not every organ has the same function, but each is necessary for the maximum health and usefulness of the body. Moreover, the whole body is animated by a common life. This is the Holy Spirit. It is His presence which makes the body one. The Church owes its coherent unity to Him. 'There is one body and one Spirit', emphasizes St. Paul (Eph. iv. 4). Even the outward, organizational divisions of the Church do not destroy its inward and spiritual unity which is indissoluble. This is 'the unity of the Spirit' or 'the fellowship of the Spirit' (Eph. iv. 3; Phil. ii. 1 and 2 Cor. xiii. 14). It is our common share in Him which makes us deeply and permanently one.

This spiritual unity, created by the One Spirit, has sometimes been termed 'the invisible Church'. Its membership is unseen. It is the community of all true believers, or, in the words of the Book of Common Prayer, 'the blessed company of all faithful people'. Every real Christian belongs to it, whatever his racial, social or ecclesiastical background. If he belongs to Christ, then he belongs to this Church.

At the same time, we cannot be content with membership of an invisible and intangible society. The invisible and universal Church has its visible and local manifestations, and to one of these every Christian must also belong. Here he will worship, and enjoy fellowship, and find opportunities for service. It will prove to be a company of sinful and fallible men and women; but he must not for that reason shun it, for he is sinful and fallible himself. He will recognize that not all its members are necessarily members of the invisible Church of Jesus Christ. Some of those whose names are inscribed on church rolls and registers have not had their names written in the Lamb's Book of Life. But it is not for him to judge. 'The Lord knows those who are his' (2 Tim. ii. 19). The minister by baptism admits into membership those who profess faith, but the Lord sees the heart. He looks not just for the external profession of faith by the lips, but for the exercise of faith by a believing heart. Such a true believer is born again by the Holy Spirit and becomes a member of the invisible, 'catholic' (i.e. universal) Church of Christ. Alas! that some who have been outwardly baptized and welcomed into visible church membership have not been born from above and received by the Lord Himself.

The Holy Spirit is not only the author of the common life of the Church, but the creator of its common love as well. The first-fruit of the Spirit is love. His very nature is love, and He imparts it to those whom He indwells. All Christians have known the remarkable experience of being drawn to other Christians whom they hardly know and whose background may be very different from their own. The relationship which exists and grows between the children of God is deeper and sweeter even than blood relationships. It is the kinship of the family of God. Truly 'we know that we have passed out of death into life, because we love the brethren' (1 Jn. ii. 14). This love is not sentimental. It is not even fundamentally emotional. Its essence is unselfishness and self-sacrifice, and it manifests itself in the desire to serve, help and enrich others. It is by love that the centrifugal force of sin is counteracted, for sin divides where love unites, and sin separates where love reconciles.

Of course the pages of the Church's history have been besmirched by many blots and smudges. Life and love have by no means always characterized the visible Church of Jesus Christ. Christians, though redeemed, are often far from perfect. Some churches appear to be dead or dying, rather than vibrant with life; and others are torn by factions and blighted by lovelessness. We have to admit that not all those who profess and call themselves Christians exhibit either the love or the life of Jesus Christ.

Nevertheless the Christian's place is in the local Christian community, however imperfect it may be, there to join with his brethren in mutual fellowship, in the worship of God, and in bearing witness to Jesus Christ in the wider world.

IV. MAN'S RESPONSE

CHAPTER IX

COUNTING THE COST

SO far we have examined some of the evidence for the unique deity of Jesus of Nazareth; we have considered man's dire need as a sinner, estranged from God, imprisoned in himself and out of harmony with his fellows; and we have outlined the main aspects of the salvation which Christ has won for us, and offers to us. It is now time for us to ask the personal question put to Jesus Christ by Saul of Tarsus on the Damascus road, 'What shall I do, Lord?', or the similar question asked by the Philippian jailor, 'What must I do to be saved?' (Acts xxii. 10, xvi. 30). Clearly we must do something. Christianity is no mere passive acquiescence in a series of propositions, however true. We may believe in the deity and the salvation of Christ, and acknowledge ourselves to be sinners in urgent need of His salvation; but all this does not make us Christian. There is a personal response which we must make to Jesus Christ, committing ourselves unreservedly to Him as our Saviour and Lord. The precise nature of this step we shall leave to the next chapter; some of its practical implications will concern us in this.

Jesus never concealed the fact that in His religion there was a demand as well as an offer. Indeed, the demand was as total as the offer was free. If He offered mankind His salvation, He demanded their submission. Jesus gave no encouragement whatever to thoughtless applicants for discipleship. He brought no pressure to bear on any enquirer. He sent irresponsible enthusiasts empty away. Luke tells us of three men who either volunteered, or were invited, to follow Jesus; but not one passed the Lord's tests (ix. 57-62). The rich young ruler, too, moral, earnest and attractive, who wanted eternal life on his own terms, went away sorrowful, with his riches intact but with neither life nor Christ as his possession.

Great multitudes were following Him one day. Perhaps they were shouting their slogans of allegiance to the Master and giving an impressive outward demonstration of their loyalty. But Christ, who could read their hearts, knew how superficial their attachment to Him was. Stopping, and turning round to speak to them, He told them a pointed parable. It was in the form of a question: 'Which of you, desiring to build a tower, does not first sit down and count the cost, whether he has enough to complete it? Otherwise, when he has laid a foundation, and is not able to finish, all who see it begin to mock him, saying, "This man began to build, and was not able to finish"' (Lk. xiv. 25-30).

The Christian landscape is strewn with the wreckage of derelict, half-built towers—the ruins of those who began to build and were unable to finish. Thousands of men and women every year are still undertaking to follow Christ without ever pausing to reflect on the cost of their enterprise. The result is the great scandal of Christendom today, so-called 'nominal Christianity'. In countries to which Christian civilization has spread, large numbers of people have covered themselves with a decent, but thin, veneer of Christianity. They have allowed themselves to become somewhat involved; enough to be respectable but not enough to be uncomfortable. Their religion is a great, soft cushion. It protects them from the hard unpleasantness of life, while changing its place and shape to suit their convenience. No wonder the cynics speak of hypocrites in the Church and dismiss religion as an escape from reality!

Very different was the message of Jesus. He never lowered His standards or modified His conditions to make His call more readily acceptable. He asked His first disciples, and He has asked every disciple since, to give Him their thoughtful and their total commitment.

We are now in a position to discuss precisely what He said. 'He called to him the multitude with his disciples, and said to them, "If any man would come after me, let him deny himself and take up his cross and follow me. For whoever would save his life will lose it; and whoever loses his life for my sake and the gospel's will save it. For what does it profit a man, to gain the whole world and forfeit his life? For what can a man give in return for his life? For whoever is ashamed of me and of my words in this adulterous and sinful generation, of him will the Son of man also be ashamed, when he comes in the glory of his Father with the holy angels" ' (Mk. viii. 34-38).

I. THE CALL TO FOLLOW CHRIST

At its simplest Christ's call was, 'Follow me.' He asked men and women for their personal allegiance. He invited them to learn from Him, to obey His words and to identify themselves with His cause.

Now there can be no following without a previous forsaking. To follow Christ is to renounce all lesser loyalties. In the days when He lived among men on earth, this meant a literal abandonment of home and work. Simon and Andrew 'left their nets and followed him'. James and John 'left their father Zebedee in the boat with the hired servants, and followed him'. Matthew, who heard Christ's call while he was 'sitting at the tax office . . . left everything, and rose and followed him' (Mk. i. 16-20; Lk. v. 27, 28).

Today, in principle, the call of the Lord Jesus has not changed. He still says, 'Follow me', and adds, 'whoever of you does not renounce all that he has cannot be my disciple' (Lk. xiv. 33). For the majority of Christians, in practice, however, this does not mean a physical departure from their home or their job. Yet it includes an inner surrender of both, and a refusal to allow either family affection or wordly ambition to occupy the first place in our hearts.

Let me be more explicit about the forsaking which cannot be separated from the following of Jesus Christ.

First, there must be *a renunciation of sin*. This, in a word, is repentance. It is the first part of Christian conversion. It can in no circumstances be bypassed. Repentance and faith belong together. We cannot follow Christ without forsaking sin. Moreover, repentance is a definite turn from every thought, word, deed and habit which is known to be wrong. It is not sufficient to feel pangs of remorse or to make some kind of apology to God. Fundamentally, repentance is a matter neither of emotion nor of speech. It is an inward change of mind and attitude towards sin which leads to a change of behaviour. There can be no compromise here. There may be sins in our lives which we do not think we ever could renounce; but we must be *willing* to let them go as we cry to God for deliverance from them. If you are in doubt regarding what is right and what wrong, what must go and what may be retained, do not be too greatly influenced by the customs and conventions of Christians of your acquaintance. Go by the clear teaching of the Bible and by the prompting of your conscience, and Christ will gradually lead you further along the path of righteousness. When He puts His finger on anything, give it up. It may be some association or recreation, some literature we read, or some attitude of pride, jealousy, or resentment, or an unforgiving spirit. Be ruthless with it. Remember what Christ taught about plucking out an offending eye or cutting off an offending limb.

Sometimes, true repentance will have to include restitution, because some of our sins affect other people as well as God. All our sins wound God, and nothing we do can heal the wound. Only the atoning death of our Saviour, Jesus Christ, can do this. But when our sins have damaged other people, we can sometimes help to repair the damage, and where we can, we must. Zacchaeus, the dishonest tax-collector, more than repaid the money he had stolen from his clients and promised to give away half his capital to the poor to compensate (no doubt) for thefts he could not repay. We must follow his example. There may be money or time for us to pay back, rumours to be contradicted, property to return, apologies to be made, or broken relationships to be mended. I do not think it is pleasing to God that we should be extravagantly scrupulous in this matter by rummaging through the years of the past and making an issue of insignificant words or deeds long ago forgotten by the offended person. But I believe we must be realistic about this duty. I have known a student rightly confess to the university authorities that she had cheated in an exam, and another return text-books which he had lifted from a shop, while an army officer wrote to the War Office with a list of items he had 'scrounged'. If we really repent, we shall want to do everything in our power to redress the past; and we cannot continue to enjoy the fruits of the sins we want to be forgiven.

Secondly, there must be *a renunciation of self*. In order to follow Christ we must not only forsake isolated sins, but renounce the very principle of self-will which lies at the root of all acts of sin. To follow Christ is to surrender to Him the rights over our own lives. It is to abdicate the throne of our heart and, putting our sceptre in His hand and our crown on His head, to do homage to Him as our King. This renunciation of self is vividly described by Jesus in three phrases.

It is to deny ourselves. 'If any man would come after me, let him deny himself.' The same verb is used of Peter's denial of the Lord in the courtyard of the high priest's palace. We are to refuse to recognize our self-centredness as absolutely as when Peter said of Christ, 'I know not the man.' Self-denial is not just giving up sweets or cigarettes for Lent. It is not to deny things to oneself, but to deny oneself to oneself. It is to say no to self, and yes to Christ; to repudiate self and acknowledge Christ.

The next phrase Jesus used is to take up the cross. 'If any man would come after me, let him deny himself and take up his cross and follow me.' If we had lived in Palestine and seen a man carrying his cross, we should at once have recognized him as a convicted prisoner being led out to pay the supreme penalty. So, says

Professor H. B. Swete in his commentary on St. Mark's Gospel, to take up the cross is 'to put oneself into the position of a condemned man on his way to execution'. The attitude to self which we are to adopt is that of crucifixion. St. Paul uses the same metaphor when he declares that 'those who belong to Christ Jesus have crucified the flesh with its passions and desires' (Gal. v. 24).

It is interesting and important to notice that in Luke's version of this saying of Christ the adverb 'daily' is added. Every day the Christian is to die. Every day he renounces the sovereignty of his own will. Every day he renews his unconditional surrender to Jesus Christ.

The third expression which Jesus used to describe the renunciation of self is to lose our life. 'Whoever loses his life . . . will save it.' The word for 'life' here means neither our physical existence, nor our soul, but our self. The *psyche* is the ego, the human personality which thinks, feels, plans and chooses. In a similar saying preserved by St. Luke Jesus simply used the reflexive pronoun and talked about a man forfeiting 'himself'. The man who commits himself to Christ, therefore, loses himself, not by the absorption of his personality in Christ's personality but by the submission of his will to Christ's will.

Thus, in order to follow Christ, we have to deny ourselves, to crucify ourselves, to lose ourselves. The full, inexorable demand of Jesus Christ is now laid bare. He does not call us to a sloppy half-heartedness, but to a vigorous, absolute commitment. He invites us to make Him our Lord. The astonishing idea is current in some circles today that we can enjoy the benefits of Christ's salvation without accepting the challenge of His sovereign lordship. Such an unbalanced notion is not to be found in the New Testament. 'Jesus is Lord' is the earliest known formulation of the creed of Christians. In days when imperial Rome was pressing its citizens to say 'Caesar is Lord', these words had a dangerous flavour. But Christians did not flinch. They could not give Caesar their first allegiance, since they served the Emperor Jesus. God had exalted His Son Jesus far above all principality and power and invested Him with a rank far superior to every rank, that before Him 'every knee should bow . . . and every tongue confess that Jesus Christ is Lord' (Phil. ii. 10, 11).

To make Christ Lord is to bring every department of our public and private lives under His control. This includes our career. God has a purpose for every life. Our business is to discover it and do it. God's plan may be different from our parents' or our own. If he is wise, the Christian will do nothing wild or reckless. He may already be engaged in, or preparing for, the work God has for him to do. But he may not. If Christ is our Lord, we must open our minds to the possibility of a change. He may call you into the ministry or on to the mission field. You must be ready to obey. Do not be in too great a hurry to discover God's will. If you are surrendered to it and waiting on God to disclose it, He will make it known to you in His own time. Whatever it proves to be, the Christian cannot be idle. Whether he is an employer, an employee or self-employed, he has a heavenly Master. He learns to see God's purpose in his work, and labours at it with all his heart, 'as serving the Lord and not men' (Col. iii. 23).

Another department of life which passes under the lordship of Jesus Christ is our marriage and our home. Jesus once said, 'Do not think that I have come to bring peace on earth; I have not come to bring peace, but a sword' (Mt. x. 34). He went on to speak of the clash of loyalties which sometimes arises within a family when one of its members begins to follow Him. Such family conflicts still take place today. The Christian should never seek them. He has a definite duty to love and honour his parents and other members of his family. He will seek peace, and will make as many concessions as he can without compromising his duty to God. Yet he can never forget Christ's word: 'He who loves father or mother . . . son or daughter more than me is not worthy of me' (Mt. x. 37). Further, a Christian is at liberty to marry only a Christian. The Bible is definite here (2 Cor. vi. 14). This command can bring great distress to somebody who is already engaged or nearly so, but the fact must be honestly faced. Marriage is the deepest possible human relationship planned by God. He designed it to be an intimate union, not only physical, emotional, intellectual and social, but spiritual. For a Christian to marry someone with whom he (or she) cannot be spiritually one is not only to disobey God but to miss the full wonder of His purpose. Indeed, so radical is true Christian conversion, that our whole attitude to marriage is likely to change, and sex, instead of being something sordid because basically selfish, becomes something sweet and beautiful because basically sacred.

Other formerly private affairs over which Jesus Christ becomes Master, when we commit our lives to Him, are our money and our time. Jesus often spoke about money, and about the danger of riches. Much of His teaching on the subject is very disturbing. It sometimes seems as if He was recommending His disciples to realize their capital and give it all away. No doubt He does call some of His followers to do this today. But for most His command is to an inner detachment rather than to a literal renunciation. The rest of the New Testament does not imply that possessions are sinful in themselves. Christ certainly meant us to put Him above material wealth just as we are to put Him above family ties. We cannot serve God and mammon. Moreover, we are to be conscientious and generous in the use of our money. It is no longer ours. We hold it in stewardship from God. The question should not now be, 'how much of my money shall I give to God?' but, 'how much of His money shall I keep for myself?'

Time is every man's problem these days; and the converted Christian will certainly have to rearrange his list of priorities. While he is a student, academic work will come high on the list. Christians should be known for their industry and honesty. But he will also make time for new employments. He will have to carve out of his busy schedule time for daily prayer and Bible reading, for setting apart Sunday as the Lord's Day which was instituted as a day of worship and rest, for fellowship with other Christians, for reading Christian literature, and for some kind of Christian service in the church or the community.

All this is involved if we are to forsake sin and self, and follow Christ.

II. THE CALL TO CONFESS CHRIST

'Whoever is ashamed of me and of my words in this adulterous and sinful generation, of him will the Son of man also be ashamed, when he comes in the glory of his Father with the holy angels.' Again, 'every one who acknowledges me before men, I also will acknowledge before my Father who is in heaven; but whoever denies me before men, I also will deny before my Father who is in heaven' (Mk. viii. 38; Mt. x. 32, 33). We are commanded not only to follow Christ privately, but to confess Him publicly. It is not enough to deny ourselves in secret if we deny Him in the open.

Now the very fact that Jesus told us not to be ashamed of Him shows that He knew we should be tempted to be ashamed; and the fact that He added 'in this adulterous and sinful generation' shows that He knew we would find it difficult. He evidently foresaw that His Church would be a minority movement in the world; and it requires courage to side with the few against the many, especially if the few are unpopular and you may not be naturally drawn to them.

Yet this open confession of Christ cannot be avoided. Paul declared it to be a condition of salvation. In order to be saved, he wrote, we have not only to believe in our hearts but to confess with our lips that Jesus is Lord, 'for man believes with his heart and so is justified, and he confesses with his lips and so is saved' (Rom. x. 9, 10). The apostle may have been referring to baptism, and certainly, if not already baptized, the convert must be baptized, partly to receive through the application of water a sign and seal of his inward cleansing, and partly to acknowledge publicly that he has trusted in Jesus Christ as his Saviour and Lord. But the Christian's open confession does not end with his baptism. He must be willing for his family and friends to know he is a Christian, both by the life he leads and by his spoken witness when a favourable opportunity occurs. He will do his utmost to be discreet and not to blunder tactlessly into the privacy of other people. At the same time, he will join a church, associate himself with other Christians in the university or at his place of business; not be afraid to own up to his Christian commitment when challenged about it, and start seeking by prayer, example and testimony to win his friends for Christ.

III. INCENTIVES

The demands which Jesus makes are heavy; but the reasons which He gives are strongly compelling. Indeed, if we are seriously to consider the total surrender for which He asks, we shall need these powerful incentives.

The first incentive is *for our own sake.* 'Whoever would save his life will lose it; and whoever loses his life . . . will save it. For what does it profit a man, to gain the whole world and forfeit his life? For what can a man give in return for his life?' (Mk. viii. 35-37). Many people have a deep-seated fear that if they commit themselves to Jesus Christ, they will lose heavily by it. They forget that Jesus came into the world that we might 'have life, and have it abundantly' (Jn. x. 10), that His purpose is to enrich not to impoverish, and that His service is perfect freedom. Of course there are losses to sustain when we submit to Christ. We have already thought of the sins and self-centredness which we must forsake; and we may lose some of our friends. But the rich and satisfying compensations far outweigh every loss. If you lose yourself by committing yourself to Christ, you will find yourself. Here is the astonishing paradox of Christian experience. True self-denial is true self-discovery. To live for ourselves is insanity and suicide; to live for God and for man is wisdom and life indeed. We do not begin to find ourselves until we have become willing to lose ourselves in the service of Christ and of our fellows.

To enforce this truth, Jesus placed in contrast the whole world and the individual soul. He then asked a business man's question touching profit and loss.

Supposing you gain the whole world and lose yourself, He asked, what profit would you have made? He was in fact arguing that on the lowest level of personal self-advantage, to follow Him is undoubtedly to have the best of the bargain, because if you do not follow Him you will lose yourself and forfeit your eternal destiny, whatever material gains you might make meanwhile. Why is this? Well, for one thing you cannot gain the whole world. For another, if you did, it would not last, and while it did last, it would not satisfy. 'What can a man give in exchange for himself?' Nothing is valuable enough even to make an offer. Of course it costs to be a Christian; but it costs more not to be.

The second incentive for Christian commitment is *for the sake of others*. We should submit to Christ not only for what we can get, but for what we can give. 'Whoever loses his life for . . . the gospel's sake, will save it.' 'For the sake of the gospel' means 'for the sake of proclaiming it to others'. We have already heard that we must not be ashamed of Christ or of His words; now we are to be positively proud of them and to spread His good news to others.

We know something of the heart-rending tragedy of this chaotic world. Our very survival is questionable. The ordinary citizen often feels a helpless victim of the tangled web of politics. What can he do? He should of course play his part in the community as a responsible citizen; but he can do more than this. It is his privilege to know in Christ the secret of peace, of personal relationships, and of changing people. He can have some share in the spreading of peace and love in the world by introducing his friends to Christ in whom alone they are to be found. The best contribution any man can make to the supply of the world's need is to live a Christian life, to build a Christian home, and thereby to radiate the light of the gospel of Jesus Christ.

The greatest incentive of all, however, is *for Christ's sake*. 'Whoever loses his life for my sake . . . will save it.' When we are asked to do some hard task, our willingness to do it depends much on who asks us. If the request comes from someone who has a claim on us, and to whom we are indebted, we are glad to comply. This is why Christ's appeal to us is so eloquent and so persuasive. He asks us to deny ourselves and follow Him for His sake. Surely this is why He describes the renunciation He demands as 'taking up the cross'. He asks no more than He gave. He asks a cross for a cross. We should follow Him neither just for what we can get nor for what we can give, but supremely because of what He gave. He gave Himself. Will it cost us much? It cost Him more. He left His Father's glory and the worship of countless angels when He came. He humbled Himself to take upon Him man's nature, to be born in a stable, to be laid in a manger, to work at a carpenter's bench, to make friends with rustic fisherfolk, to die on a common cross, and to bear the sins of the world.

Only a sight of the cross will make us willing to deny ourselves and follow Him. Our little crosses are eclipsed by His. If we once catch a glimpse of the greatness of His love to suffer such shame and pain for us who deserved nothing but judgment, only one course of action will seem to be left. How can we deny or reject such a Lover?

If, then, you suffer from moral anaemia, take my advice and steer clear of Christianity. If you want to live a life of easygoing self-indulgence, whatever you do, do not become a Christian. But if you want a life of self-discovery, deeply satisfying to the nature God has given you; if you want a life of adventure in which you have the privilege of serving Him and your fellow men; if you want a life in which to express something of the overwhelming gratitude you are beginning to feel for Him who died for you, then I urge you to yield your life, without reserve and without delay, to your Lord and Saviour, Jesus Christ.

> Thou callest clear, cold centuries across,
> And bidd'st me follow Thee, and take my cross,
> And daily lose myself, myself deny,
> And stern against myself shout 'Crucify'.

My stubborn nature rises to rebel
Against Thy call. Proud choruses of hell
Unite to magnify my restless hate
Of servitude, lest I capitulate.

The world, to see my cross, would pause and jeer.
I have no choice, but still to persevere
To save myself—and follow Thee from far,
More slow than Magi—for I have no star.

And yet Thou callest still. Thy cross
Eclipses mine, transforms the bitter loss
I thought that I would suffer if I came
To Thee,—into immeasurable gain.

I kneel before Thee, Jesus, crucified,
My cross is shouldered and my self denied;
I'll follow daily, closely—will not flee
To lose myself, for love of man and Thee.

CHAPTER X

MAKING A DECISION

THAT a decision is necessary in order to become a Christian is an idea quite foreign to many people. Some imagine that they are already Christians because they have been born in a Christian country. 'After all', they say, 'we are neither Jews, nor Mohammedans, nor Buddhists; presumably we are Christians therefore!' Others suppose that, having received a Christian education, and having been taught to accept the Christian creed and Christian standards of behaviour, nothing further is required of them. But whatever his parentage and upbringing, every responsible adult is obliged to make up his own mind for or against Christ. We cannot remain neutral. Nor can we drift into Christianity. Nor can anybody else settle the matter for us. We must decide for ourselves.

Even agreement with all that has so far been written in this book is not sufficient. We may concede that the evidence for Christ's deity is strong, and that He is in fact the Son of God; we may believe that He came and died to be the Saviour of the world; we may also admit that we are sinners and need such a Saviour. But none of these things makes us Christians, nor do all of them together. Intellectual assent is one thing; moral decision is another. To believe certain facts about the person and work of Christ is a necessary preliminary, but true faith will translate such mental belief into a decisive act of trust. Intellectual conviction must lead to personal commitment.

I used myself to think that because Jesus had died on the cross, by some kind of rather mechanical transaction the whole world had been automatically saved. I remember how puzzled, even indignant, I was when it was first suggested to me that I needed to appropriate Christ and His salvation for myself. Thank God, I came to see that, though an acknowledgement that I needed *a* Saviour was good, and a belief that Christ was *the* Saviour of the world was better, best of all was a personal acceptance of Him as *my* Saviour. Certainly the personal pronoun is prominent in the Bible. 'The Lord is *my* shepherd, I shall not want.' 'The Lord is *my* light and *my* salvation.' 'O God, thou art *my* God.' 'The surpassing worth of knowing Christ Jesus *my* Lord' (see Pss. xxiii. 1, xxvii. 1, lxiii. 1; Phil. iii. 8).

There is one verse in the Bible which seems to make more clear than any other the decision which has to be made and the step which has to be taken. It is a verse universally beloved by Christians. It has been used by God to very many seekers. It is the verse which brought me to Christ. It contains words of Christ Himself: 'Behold, I stand at the door and knock; if any one hears my voice and opens the door, I will come in to him and eat with him, and he with me' (Rev. iii. 20).

The human heart or soul is here likened to a house. Each of us has his own life to live, his own house to manage. I am king of my castle; you are king of yours. Moreover, the precincts of our castle are sacred and guarded, and no one shall be permitted to intrude without our express permission. Outside the front door of the house of our personality stands the Lord Jesus Christ, knocking. He wants to come in. The decision we have to make is quite simple: shall we let Him in or keep Him out?

Holman Hunt, the well-known pre-Raphaelite artist, has made this verse live to many people by his picture 'The Light of the World'. The original, painted in 1853 and exhibited in the Royal Academy in 1854, was bequeathed to Keble College, Oxford, by Thomas Combe of the Oxford University Press, and hangs in the College Chapel. The painting which can be seen in the south aisle of St. Paul's cathedral is a replica which the artist himself made forty years after the original.

On 5 May 1854 *The Times* published a letter from John Ruskin in which the picture was described. ' . . . On the left-hand side of the picture is seen this door of the human soul. It is fast barred; its bars and nails are rusty; it is knitted and bound to its stanchions by creeping tendrils of ivy, showing that it has never been opened. A bat hovers about it; its threshold is overgrown with brambles, nettles, and fruitless corn. . . . Christ approaches it in the night-time. . . . ' Christ is invested with a royal robe and wears the crown of thorns. In His left hand He holds a lantern, because He is the light of the world, while His right hand is raised to knock at the door.

I propose that, in order to clarify the decision which we have to make, we should ask a number of questions about this house, its occupant, and its visitor.

First, *who lives in the house?* Perhaps the best answer is 'everyman'. The house is representative of every human heart and life, and the occupant is the individual you or I. But what are we like, and why should Jesus Christ visit us? We are sinners, and He visits us because we are sinners. He has come to our door not because we are worthy that He should call on us, but because we need Him.

The context in which this verse is embedded is illuminating. The second and third chapters of the Revelation comprise letters which were dictated by the ascended Christ to St. John for transmission to seven of the principal churches of Asia. The verse we are considering is to be found at the end of the last letter. This is addressed to the church of Laodicea. Now Laodicea was a prosperous city in those days. It was renowned in particular for its manufacture of clothing from the wool of local sheep, its medical school where the famous Phrygian eye powder was made, and its wealthy banks. Material prosperity had brought in its wake a spirit of self-satisfaction and complacency which had even contaminated the Christian church. Attached to the local Christian assembly were professing Christians who proved to be Christian in name only. They were tolerably respectable, but nothing more. Their religious interest was shallow and casual. In the language of Jesus they were neither cold, nor hot, but lukewarm, and therefore distasteful to Him. Their spiritual tepidity seems to have been due to the fact that they were

deluded. They had far too high an opinion of themselves. They must have been shocked to read Christ's
word to them: 'You say, "I am rich, I have prospered,
and I need nothing"; not knowing that you are
wretched, pitiable, poor, blind, and naked' (iii. 17).

What a description of proud and prosperous Laodicea!
They were naked, blind beggars—naked despite their
clothing factory, blind despite their Phrygian eye-salve,
and beggars despite their banks. We are no different.
Perhaps we say, as they did, 'I need nothing.' It would
be hard to find any words more spiritually dangerous.
It is our arrogant, self-contained independence which,
more than anything else, keeps us from committing ourselves to Christ. Of course we need Him! Without Him
we are morally naked (with no clothing to fit us for
God's presence), blind to spiritual truth, and beggars,
having no currency with which to purchase the favour
of heaven. But Christ can clothe us with His righteousness, touch our eyes into sight, and enrich us with
spiritual wealth. Apart from Him, and until we open
the door to admit Him, we are like blind and naked
beggars.

Secondly, *who is the visitor?* It is the historic Jesus.
He is no figment of the imagination, no fictitious character from a religious novel. This is the man of Nazareth,
whose claims, character and resurrection warrant the
conclusion that He is the Son of God. Moreover, He is
the crucified Saviour. The hand that knocks is scarred.
The feet which stand on the threshold still bear the
print of nails. This is the One who died for our sins on
the cross. He is also the risen Christ. John has already
described in the first chapter of the Revelation the
glorified Lord whom he saw in a vision. His eyes were
like flaming fire and His feet like burnished brass. His
voice thundered like the sound of many waters and His
face was radiant like the sun shining in full strength.
These features describe in vivid symbolism the risen
glory of Jesus Christ. No wonder John fell at His feet.
It is hard to understand how a majestic person like
Him could ever deign to visit poor, blind and naked
beggars like us.

Thirdly, *what is He doing?* He is standing. The Greek tense is a perfect. It indicates that He has come and stood, and is still standing. Further, the preposition means 'up to'. He has come close to the door. He is no distance away. He might have sat on His throne in regal pomp and waited for us to come to Him. Instead, He has come to us, to our very doorstep. Perhaps He first came long ago. How many years have you kept Him waiting?

He is not only standing; He is knocking. This is a present tense. He came and stood. He is continuously knocking. He leaves us in no doubt either of His presence or of His purpose.

Next, He is speaking. He says: 'Behold, I stand at the door and knock.' He draws our attention to His visit. He asks us to notice that He is there.

All three verbs lay emphasis on Christ's humility and man's freedom. He is standing at the door, not kicking at it. He is knocking at the door, not pushing it. He is speaking to us, not shouting. Yet the house is His! He is the architect; He designed it. He is the builder; He made it. He is the landlord; He bought it with the price of His life-blood. It is His by right of plan, construction and purchase. We are only tenants in a house which does not belong to us. He could put His shoulder to the door; He prefers to put His hand to the knocker. He could command us to open to Him; instead, He merely invites us to do so. He stands patiently; He knocks gently; He speaks softly. He forces an entry into nobody's life. He says (verse 18) 'I counsel you . . . '. He has a right to issue orders; He is content to give advice. Such are His gracious condescension and humility, and the freedom He has given us which He refuses to compel.

Fourthly, *what does He want to do?* He wants to come in. That is why He stands at the door, not the window. He is not satisfied to look in. He can do that in any case. Polite conversation will not deceive Him. He asks for much more than a distant nodding acquaintance. We must make a decision to open the door and ask Him to come in. It may stretch our credulity to breaking point, but it is this that He wants to do. He who does not live in temples made with hands, and whom the heavens and the heaven of heavens cannot contain, will yet stoop to enter the mean hovel of our sinful hearts.

But why does He wish to come in? We have already seen why. He wants to be both our Saviour and our Lord. He died to be our Saviour. If we receive Him, He will be able to apply the benefits of His death to us personally. Once inside the house, His first task will be to springclean it. He will renovate, redecorate and refurnish it. In other words, He will cleanse and forgive us, and all the past will be blotted out. Moreover, He promises to sup with us and to permit us to sup with Him. The phrase describes the unutterable joy of His friendship. He not only gives Himself to us but desires that we should give ourselves to Him. We have been strangers; but now we are friends. There has been a closed door between us; but now we are seated at the same table.

> How marvellous that I, a filthy clod,
> May yet hold converse with my God![1]

He will enter also as our Lord and Master. Our house will come under His management. He will take over the control of it. There is no sense in opening the door unless we are willing for this. As He steps across the threshold, we must hand Him our whole bunch of keys, so that He may have free access into every room. We can have no Bluebeard's chamber locked against Him. A fourth year Canadian student once wrote to me: 'Instead of giving Christ a whole set of different keys to the many rooms of the house . . . I have given him a pass key to the whole lot.'

We must therefore truly repent, turning resolutely from everything we know to be displeasing to Him. I do not mean that we are to make ourselves better before we invite Him in. On the contrary, it is because we cannot forgive or improve ourselves, that we need Him to come to us. But we must be willing for Him to do what rearranging He likes when He has come in. There can

[1] Angelus Silesius.

be no resistance. We must surrender absolutely and unconditionally to the lordship of Jesus Christ. We cannot make our own terms. What will this involve? In detail I cannot tell you. In principle, it means a determination to forsake evil and follow Christ.

Do you hesitate? Do you say it is unreasonable to submit to Christ in the dark? Surely it is not. It is much more reasonable than marriage. In marriage a man and a woman commit themselves to each other without condition. They do not know what the future holds for them. But they love each other, and they trust each other. So they promise to take each other, 'to have and to hold from this day forward, for better for worse, for richer for poorer, in sickness and in health, to love and to cherish, till death us do part'. If humans can thus trust humans, can we not trust God's Son? It is more reasonable to commit oneself to the divine Christ than to the finest and noblest of mortals. He will never betray or abuse your confidence.

Fifthly, *what must we do?* To begin with, we must hear His voice. It is tragically possible to turn a deaf ear to Him and to drown the insistent whisper of His appeal. Sometimes we hear His voice through the prickings of the conscience and sometimes through the gropings of the mind. Now it is a moral defeat, now an inexplicable spiritual hunger, now sickness or suffering or fear, through which we detect His pleading. We can listen to His call through a friend or a preacher or a book. When we hear, we must listen. 'He that hath ears to hear', said Jesus, 'let him hear.'

Next, we must open the door. Having heard His voice, we must open to His knock. To open the door to Jesus Christ is a pictorial way of describing an act of faith in Him as our Saviour and an act of submission to Him as our Lord.

It is a definite act. The tense of the Greek verb makes this clear. The door does not happen to swing open by chance. Nor is it already ajar. It is closed, and it needs to be opened. Moreover, Christ cannot open the door. There is neither handle nor latch on the door in Holman Hunt's picture. It is said that he omitted them deliberately because the handle is on the inside of the door. Christ knocks; but we must open.

It is an individual act. Jesus says, 'If anyone hears my voice, and opens the door, I will come into him.' Every man must make his own decision and take this step himself. Nobody else can do it for you. Christian parents and teachers, ministers and friends can point the way, but your hand and only yours can draw back the bolts and turn the handle.

It is a unique act. You can take this step only once. When Christ has entered, He will bolt and bar the door on the inside. Sin may drive Him into the cellar or the attic, but He will never altogether abandon the house He has entered. 'I will never fail you nor forsake you,' He says (Heb. xiii. 5). I did not say that you would emerge from this experience with the fully grown wings of an angel! On the contrary, you will not become perfect in the twinkling of an eye. You can become a Christian in a moment, but not a mature Christian. Christ can enter, and cleanse and forgive you, in a matter of seconds, but it may take a lifetime for your character to be transformed and moulded to His will. It takes only a few minutes for a bride and bridegroom to be married, but in the rough-and-tumble of their home it may take years for two strong wills to be dove-tailed into one. So commitment to Christ is almost instantaneous, while adjustment to Him will continue and increase.

It is a deliberate act. You do not have to wait for a supernatural light to flash upon you from heaven, or for an emotional experience to overtake you. No. Christ came into the world and died for your sins. He has now come and stood outside the front door of the house of your life, and He is knocking. He can do no more. The next move is yours. His hand is already on the knocker; your hand must now feel for the latch.

It is an urgent act. Do not wait longer than you must. Time is passing. The future is uncertain. You may never have a better opportunity than this. 'Do not boast about tomorrow, for you do not know what a day may bring forth.' 'The Holy Spirit says, "Today, when you hear

his voice, do not harden your hearts . . . " ' (Pr. xxvii.
1; Heb. iii. 7, 8). Do not delay until you have tried to
make yourself better, or worthier of Christ's entry; or
until you have solved all your problems. If you believe
that Christ is the Son of God and that He died to be
your Saviour, that is enough. The rest will follow in due
time. True, there is danger in rash and precipitate
action; but there is equal danger in procrastination. If
in your heart of hearts you know you should act, then
I urge you to put it off no longer.

It is an indispensable act. Of course there is much
more to the Christian life than this. As we shall see in
the next chapter, there is getting into the fellowship of
the Church, discovering and doing God's will, growing
in grace and understanding, and undertaking some work
for Christ; but this step is the beginning, and nothing
else will do instead. You can believe in Christ intellectually and admire Him; you can say your prayers to
Him through the keyhole (I did for many years); you
can push coins at Him under the door; you can be
moral, decent, upright and good; you can be religious
and pious; you can have been baptized and confirmed;
you can be deeply versed in the philosophy of religion;
you can be a theological student and even an ordained
minister—and still not have opened the door to Christ.
There is no substitute for this.

A University Professor describes in his autobiography
how he was travelling one day on the top of a bus when
'without words and (I think) almost without images, a
fact about myself was somehow presented to me. I
became aware that I was holding something at bay, or
shutting something out. Or, if you like, that I was
wearing some stiff clothing, like corsets, or even a suit
of armour, as if I were a lobster. I felt myself being,
there and then, given a free choice. I could open the
door or keep it shut; I could unbuckle the armour or
keep it on. Neither choice was presented as a duty; no
threat or promise was attached to either, though I knew
that to open the door or to take off the corset meant
the incalculable. . . . I chose to open, to unbuckle, to
loosen the rein. I say "I chose", yet it did not really

seem possible to do the opposite.' So Professor C. S. Lewis describes his experience in *Surprised by Joy*.

A titled lady went forward in the Harringay arena at Dr. Billy Graham's invitation. In the counselling room she was introduced to an adviser who, discovering that she had not yet committed her life to Christ, suggested that she should pray there and then. Bowing her head, she said, 'Dear Lord Jesus, I want You to come into my heart more than anything else in all the world. Amen'.

A boy in his later teens knelt at his bedside one Sunday night in the dormitory of his public school. It was about 10 p.m. on 13 February 1938. In a simple, matter-of-fact but definite way he told Christ that he had made rather a mess of his life so far; he confessed his sins; he thanked Christ for dying for him; and he asked Him to come into his life. The following day he wrote in his diary: 'Yesterday really *was* an eventful day! . . . Up till now Christ has been on the circumference and I have but asked Him to guide me instead of giving Him complete control. Behold! He stands at the door and knocks. I have heard Him and now is He come into my house. He has cleansed it and now rules therein. . . . ' And the day after: 'I really have felt an immense and new joy throughout today. It is the joy of being at peace with the world and of being in touch with God. How well do I know now that He rules me and that I never really knew Him before. . . . '

These are extracts from my own diary. I venture to quote them because I did not want you to think that I was recommending you to take a step which I had not taken myself.

Are you a Christian? a real and committed Christian? Your answer depends on another question—not whether you go to church or not, believe the creed or not, or lead a decent life or not (important as all these are in their place), but rather on this: Which side of the door is Jesus Christ? Is He inside or outside? That is the crucial issue.

Perhaps you are ready to make a decision and thoughtfully to open the door to Christ. If you are not sure if you have ever done so, I advise you to make sure. It may be, as someone has put it, that you will be going over in ink what you have already written in pencil. I want to suggest that you get away and alone to pray. Confess your sins, and forsake them. Thank Christ for His death for your sake and in your place. Then open the door and ask Him to come in as your own personal Saviour and Lord. You might find it a help to echo in your heart this prayer:

'Lord Jesus, I admit that I am a sinner. I have sinned in thought, word and deed. I am sorry for my sins, and I turn from them in repentance.

'I believe that You died for me, bearing my sins in Your own body. I thank You for Your great love.

'Now I open the door. Come in, Lord Jesus. Come in as my Saviour, to cleanse me. Come in as my Lord and Master, to take control of me. And I will serve You, in fellowship with other Christians, as You give me strength, all my life. Amen.'

If you have prayed this prayer, and meant it, quietly and humbly thank Christ that He has come in. He said He would. He has pledged His word: 'If any one hears my voice and opens the door, *I will come in* to him. . . . ' Disregard your feelings; trust His promise; and thank Him that He has kept His word.

CHAPTER XI

BEING A CHRISTIAN[1]

THIS last chapter is written for those who have opened the door of their heart and soul to Jesus Christ. They have committed themselves to Him. They have thus begun the Christian life. But *becoming* a Christian is one thing; *being* a Christian is another. It is with the implications of being a Christian that we must now concern ourselves.

You took a simple step; you simply invited Christ to come in as your Saviour and Lord. But then God performed a stupendous miracle. He gave you a new life. You were born again. You entered the family of God. You became a child of God. You may not have been conscious of any great change, even as at the time of your physical birth you were not conscious of what had taken place. Nevertheless, just as when you were born you emerged as a new independent personality, so when you were born again you became spiritually a new creature in Christ.

But (you may be thinking) is not God the Father of all men? Are not all people the children of God? No! The Bible clearly distinguishes between a general paternity of God which extends over all whom He has made, and a restricted fatherhood which is enjoyed by those whom He has remade in Christ. He is the Creator of all; but He is the Father only of those who have trusted in Jesus Christ as their Saviour. St. John explains this in the prologue to his Gospel when he writes: 'He (that is, Jesus) came to his own home, and his own people received him not. But to all who received him, who believed in his name, he gave power to become children of God; who were born . . . of God' (Jn. i. 11-13). The three clauses beginning with the relative

[1] This chapter has been published separately in booklet form (Inter-Varsity Fellowship, 3d.).

pronoun 'who' all describe the same people. The children of God are those who are born of God; and those who are born of God are those who have received Christ into their lives and who have believed in His name.

If then we want to understand what, according to the Bible, it means to be a Christian, we must grasp the privileges and responsibilities of the child of God.

1. THE PRIVILEGES OF THE CHILD OF GOD

The unique privilege of the child of God, who has been born of God, is that he is related to God. Let us consider this relationship.

a. An intimate relationship

We have already seen in this book that we were separated from God. Our sins had alienated us from Him. They had come as a barrier between us and Him. But now the barrier has been thrown down. Like clouds they had blotted out the sunshine of His face. But now the clouds have lifted and the sun is shining. To use another analogy common particularly in St. Paul's Epistles, we were under the just condemnation of the Judge of all the earth; but now through Jesus Christ (who bore our condemnation and to whom we have become united by faith) we have been 'justified', that is, brought into acceptance with God and pronounced righteous. Our Judge has become our Father.

'See what love the Father has given us, that we should be called children of God; and so we are' (1 Jn. iii. 1). 'Father' and 'Son' are the distinctive titles which Jesus gave to God and to Himself, and they are the very names which He permits us to use! By union with Him we are permitted to share His own intimate relation to the Father. Cyprian, Bishop of Carthage in the middle of the third century AD, well expresses our privilege in his treatise on the Lord's Prayer: 'How great is the Lord's indulgence! How great are His condescension and plenteousness of goodness towards us, seeing that He has wished us to pray in the sight of God in such a way as

to call God Father, and to call ourselves sons of God,
even as Christ is the Son of God—a name which none
of us would dare to venture on in prayer, unless He
Himself had allowed us thus to pray.'

Now at last we can repeat the Lord's Prayer without
hypocrisy. Previously the words had a hollow sound; now
they ring with new and noble meaning. God is indeed
our Father in heaven, who knows our necessities before
we ask and will not fail to give good things to His
children (Mt. vi. 32, vii. 11). He may need to chasten
and correct us, 'for the Lord disciplines him whom he
loves, and chastises every son whom he receives' (Heb. xii.
6, quoted from Pr. iii. 12), but the rod is wielded by
a loving Father's hand. With such a Father, gracious,
wise and strong, we can be delivered from all our fears.

b. An assured relationship

The Christian's relationship to God as a child to his
Father is not only intimate, but sure. How then can we
know that it has been established? So many people seem
to do no more than hope for the best; is it possible to
know for certain? It is. It is more than possible; it is
God's revealed will for us. We ought to be sure of our
relationship with God not just for the sake of our own
peace of mind and helpfulness to others, but because
God means us to be sure. St. John states categorically
that this was his purpose in writing his first general
Epistle. 'I write this to you who believe in the name of
the Son of God, that you may know that you have
eternal life' (1 Jn. v. 13).

Yet the way to *be* sure is not just to *feel* sure. Most
young Christians, at the beginning of their Christian life,
make this mistake. They rely too much on their
superficial feelings. One day they *feel* close to God; the
next day they *feel* estranged from Him again. They
imagine that their feelings accurately reflect their
spiritual condition, and so they fall into a frenzy of
uncertainty. Their Christian life becomes a precarious
switchback ride as they soar to the heights of elation,
only to plunge again into the depths of depression. This
is no good at all. Do learn to mistrust your feelings.

They are so variable. They change with the weather and vacillate with our health. We are fickle creatures of whim and mood, and our fluctuating feelings very often have nothing whatever to do with our spiritual progress.

The basis of our knowledge that we are in relationship with God is not our feelings, but the fact that He says we are. The test we are to apply to ourselves is objective rather than subjective. We are not to grub around inside ourselves for evidence of spiritual life, but to look up and out and away to God and His word. But where shall we find God's word to assure us that we are His children?

(i) *God's word is written in our Bibles*. God promises in His written word to give eternal life to those who receive Christ. 'This is the testimony, that God gave us eternal life, and this life is in his Son. He who has the Son has life; he who has not the Son has not life' (1 Jn. v. 11, 12). Humbly to believe that we have eternal life is not then presumptuous. On the contrary, to believe God's word is humility, not pride, and wisdom, not presumption. The folly and the sin would be to doubt, for 'he who does not believe God, has made him a liar, because he has not believed in the testimony that God has borne to his son' (1 Jn. v. 10). Now the Bible is full of God's promises. The sensible Christian begins as soon as possible to store them in his memory. Then when he falls into the ditch of depression and doubt, he can haul himself out with the chains of divine promise. Here are some promises to start memorizing: Jn. vi. 37, x. 28; 1 Cor. x. 13; Heb. xiii. 5, 6; Is. xli. 10; Jas. i. 5; 1 Jn. i. 9.[1]

(ii) *God's word is heard in our hearts*. Listen to these statements. 'God's love has been poured into our hearts through the Holy Spirit . . . ' and 'When we cry, "Abba! Father!" it is the Spirit himself bearing witness with our spirit that we are the children of God' (Rom. v. 5, viii. 15, 16). Every Christian knows what this means.

[1] See also *Some Basic Texts* (Inter-Varsity Fellowship, 6d.), a classified selection of some one hundred and fifty Scripture passages for memorizing.

The outward witness of the Holy Spirit in Scripture is confirmed by the inward witness of the Holy Spirit in experience. This is not to place any confidence in our shallow and changeable feelings; it is rather to expect a deepening conviction in our hearts as the Holy Spirit assures us of God's love for us and prompts us to cry 'Father!' as we seek God's face in prayer.

(iii) *God's word is seen in our lives.* The same Spirit who bears witness to our sonship in Scripture and experience completes His testimony in our character. If we have been born again into God's family, then God's Spirit dwells within us; and He will not have indwelt us long before He begins to work a change in our manner of life. St. John applies this test ruthlessly in his first Epistle. If any man continues to disobey the commandments of God and to disregard his duties to his fellow men, he is not a Christian, whatever his profession may be. Righteousness of life and practical love to one's neighbours, specially to one's Christian brethren, are indispensable marks of the child of God.

c. A secure relationship

Supposing we have entered this intimate relationship with God, and are assured of it by God's own word, is it a secure relationship? Or can we be born into God's family one moment and repudiated from it the next? The Bible indicates that it is a permanent relationship. 'If children, then heirs,' wrote St. Paul, 'heirs of God and fellow heirs with Christ' (Rom. viii. 17).

'But what happens if and when I sin?' you may ask. 'Do I not then forfeit my sonship and cease to be God's child?' No. Think of the analogy of a human family. A young man is rude to his parents. A cloud descends on the home. There is tension in the atmosphere. Father and son are not on speaking terms. What has happened? Has the boy ceased to be a son? No. Their relationship has not changed; it is their fellowship which has been spoiled. Relationship depends on birth; fellowship depends on behaviour. As soon as the young man apologizes, he is forgiven. And forgiveness restores fellowship. Meanwhile, his relationship has remained the same. He may have been temporarily a disobedient, and even a defiant, son; but he has not ceased to be a son.

So it is with the children of God. When we sin, we do not forfeit our relationship to Him as children, though our fellowship with Him is marred until we confess and forsake our sin. As soon as we 'confess our sins, he is faithful and just, and will forgive our sins and cleanse us from all unrighteousness', for 'if any one does sin, we have an advocate with the Father, Jesus Christ the righteous; and he is the expiation for our sins' (1 Jn. i. 9, ii. 1, 2). So when you fall, fall on your knees and humbly seek your Father's forgiveness at once. Keep short accounts with Him. Aim to preserve your conscience clear and undefiled.

Put in another way, we can only be justified once; but we need to be forgiven every day. When Jesus washed the feet of His disciples, He gave them an illustration of this truth. Peter asked Him to wash his hands and his head as well as his feet. But Jesus replied: 'He who has bathed does not need to wash, except for his feet, but he is clean all over' (Jn. xiii. 9, 10). A man invited to a dinner party in Jerusalem would take a bath before going out. On arrival at his friend's house, he would not be offered another bath; but a slave would meet him at the front door and wash his feet. So when we first come to Christ in repentance and faith, we receive a 'bath' (which is justification, and is outwardly symbolized in baptism). It never needs to be repeated. But as we walk through the dusty streets of this world, we constantly need to 'have our feet washed' (which is daily forgiveness).

II. THE RESPONSIBILITIES OF THE CHILD OF GOD

To be a child of God is a great and wonderful privilege, but it also carries with it definite obligations. St. Peter implies this when he writes: 'As newborn babes, desire the sincere milk of the word, that ye may grow thereby'

(1 Pet. ii. 2 AV). The great privilege of the child of God is relationship; his great responsibility is growth. Everybody loves children, but nobody in his right mind wants them to stay in the nursery. The tragedy, however, is that many Christians, born again in Christ, never grow up. Others even suffer from infantile regression of the spirit. Our heavenly Father's purpose, on the other hand, is that 'babes in Christ' should become 'mature in Christ' (1 Cor. iii. 1; Col. i. 28). Our birth must be followed by growth. The crisis of justification (our acceptance before God) must lead to the process of sanctification (our growth in holiness).

There are two main spheres in which the Christian is meant to grow. The first is in understanding and the second in holiness. When he begins the Christian life, he probably understands very little and he has only just come to know God. Now he must increase in the knowledge of God and of his Lord and Saviour, Jesus Christ (Col. i. 10; 2 Pet. iii. 18). This knowledge is partly intellectual and partly personal. In connection with the former, I would urge you not only to study the Bible but to read good Christian books.[1] To neglect to grow in your understanding is to court disaster. The Christian way is strewn with such casualties.

We must also grow in holiness of life. The New Testament writers speak of the development of our faith in God, our love for our fellow men and our likeness to Christ. Every son of God longs to become more and more conformed in his character and behaviour to the Son of God Himself. The Christian life is a life of righteousness. We must seek to obey God's commandments and do God's will. The Holy Spirit has been given us for this purpose. He has made our bodies His temple. He dwells within us. And as we allow Him

---

[1] I suggest as a beginning *Mere Christianity*, by C. S. Lewis, which is an introduction to Christian theology, ethics and apologetics; *Henceforth*, by H. A. Evan Hopkins, or *The Way*, by Stephen Winward and Godfrey Robinson, both of which give much practical advice on how to make progress in the Christian life; and *Hudson Taylor—The Growth of a Soul*, by Dr. and Mrs. Howard Taylor, one of the most inspiring Christian biographies ever written.

continuously to fill us with His power, He will subdue our evil desires and cause His fruit to appear, which is 'love, joy, peace, patience, kindness, goodness, faithfulness, gentleness, self-control' (Gal. v. 16, 22, 23).

But how shall we grow? What are the secrets of success? There are three, which are the major responsibilities of the child of God.

a. Our Duty to God

Our relationship to our heavenly Father, though secure, is not static. He ardently desires that His children shall grow up to know Him more and more intimately. Generations of Christians have discovered that the only way to do so is to make time to wait upon Him every day. What many people call the daily 'quiet times', first thing in the morning and last thing at night, are an indispensable necessity for the Christian who wants to make progress. We are all busy nowadays, but we must somehow rearrange our priorities in order to make time for this. It will mean rigorous self-discipline, but granted this, together with a legible Bible and an alarm clock that works, we are well on the road to victory.

A balanced quiet time will include both Bible reading and prayer—Bible reading because through it God speaks to us, and prayer because by it we speak to God. It is important to be systematic in the reading of the Bible. Various methods are available to help you.[1] Pray before you read, asking the Holy Spirit to open your eyes and illumine your mind. Then read slowly, meditatively and thoughtfully. Read and re-read the passage. Learn to ruminate in the pastures of God's Word. Wrestle with it till it yields its meaning. This may necessitate consulting a modern translation or a good commentary. Then go on to apply to your own circumstances the message of the verses you have read.

---

[1] I recommend the Scripture Union, 3-5 Wigmore Street, W.1; and, for students, the I.V.F. books *Light on the Way*, *Hold the Faith* (introductory courses) and *Search the Scriptures* (a three-year study course). The I.V.F. booklet *The Quiet Time* has some very valuable advice about daily prayer and Bible reading.

Look for promises to claim and commands to obey, examples to follow and sins to avoid. It is a great help to keep a notebook and write down what you learn. Above all, look for Jesus Christ. He is the chief subject of the Bible. We can not only find Him revealed there, but can meet Him personally through its pages.

Prayer follows naturally. Begin by speaking back to God on the same subject on which He has spoken to you. Don't change the conversation! If He has spoken to you of Himself and His glory, worship Him. If He has spoken to you of yourself and your sins, confess them. Thank Him for any blessings which may have been revealed in the passage, and pray that its lessons may be learned by yourself and your friends. When you have prayed over the Bible passage you have read, you will want to go on with other prayers. If your Bible is the first great aid to prayer, your diary will be the second. Commit to Him in the morning all the details of the day which lies before you, and in the evening run through the day again, confessing the sins you have committed, giving thanks for the blessings you have received and praying for the people you have met. God is your Father. Be natural, confidential and bold. He is interested in all the details of your life. Very soon you will find it essential to start some kind of prayer list of your relatives and friends for whom you feel a responsibility to pray. It is wise to make your list as flexible as possible, so that people can be easily added to it or taken from it.

b. *Our Duty to the Church*

The Christian life is not just our own private affair. If we have been born again into God's family, not only has He become our Father but every other Christian believer in the world, whatever his nation or denomination, has become our brother or sister in Christ. One of the commonest names for Christians in the New Testament is 'brethren'. This is a glorious truth. But it is no good supposing that membership of the universal Church of Christ is enough; we must belong to some local branch of it. Nor is it sufficient to be a member of a Christian Union (although I hope you will become active in yours). Every Christian's place is in a local church (or in his college chapel) sharing in its worship, its fellowship and its witness. Baptism is the way of entry into such a visible Christian society. It has other meanings as well, but if you have not been baptized, you should ask your minister or chaplain to baptize you. Then do allow yourself to be drawn right into the Christian fellowship. Much may seem strange to you at first, but do not stand aside. Church or chapel attendance on Sundays is a definite Christian duty, and nearly every branch of the Christian Church agrees that the Lord's Supper or Holy Communion is the central service of the Church, for in it we commemorate our Saviour's death in fellowship with one another. I hope I am not giving the impression that fellowship is merely a Sunday treat! 'Philadelphia', the love of the brethren, is a new word in the Christian's vocabulary, and he will discover new depths of friendship in the Christian brotherhood. His closest friends will inevitably be Christians and, above all, his life-partner must be a Christian too (2 Cor. vi. 14).

c. Our Duty to the World

The Christian life is a family affair, in which the children enjoy sweet fellowship with their Father and with each other, but let it not for one moment be thought that this exhausts their responsibilities. Christians are not a self-regarding coterie of smug and selfish prigs, who are interested only in themselves. On the contrary, every true Christian is deeply concerned about those of his fellow men who are still outside the Church. The Bible calls them 'the world'. They have not yet entered God's family. Perhaps God will call you into the ministry of the gospel or to go overseas as a missionary. There is no greater privilege this side of heaven than such service. The world is still waiting to be evangelized. Millions of people have never heard of Jesus Christ and His salvation. For centuries the Church has slumbered. Is this the generation in which Christians will awake and win the world for Christ? Perhaps He has a special task for you to do. If you are a student already launched on your course, it would be quite wrong for you to do anything rash or hasty. But do seek to discover God's will for your life, and be surrendered to it.

Although every Christian is not called to be a minister or a missionary, God does intend every Christian to be a witness to Jesus Christ. In his own home, among his friends, in his college or at his place of business, it is his solemn responsibility to seek to win other people for Christ. He will be humble, discreet and courteous, but determined. The way to begin is by prayer. Ask God to give you a special concern for one or two of your friends. It is usually wise to keep to people of your own sex and about your own age. Then pray regularly and definitely for their conversion; foster your friendship with them; take trouble to spend time with them; and really love them for themselves. Soon an opportunity will come to take them to some service or meeting where they will hear the gospel explained; or to give them some Christian literature to read; or to tell them simply what Jesus Christ has come to mean to you and how you found Him. I need hardly say that our most eloquent testimony will be without effect if we are contradicting it by our example; while little is more influential for Christ than a life which He is transforming.

Such are the great privileges and responsibilities of the child of God. Born into the family of God and enjoying with his heavenly Father a relationship which is intimate, assured and secure, he is disciplined in his daily quiet times, loyal in his church membership, and active in seeking, by his prayers and his personal testimony, to win his friends for Christ.

Yet all the time he knows that fundamentally he no longer belongs to this world. Although he has definite duties as a Christian citizen, he is at the same time a stranger and a pilgrim on earth, journeying to his eternal home in heaven. So he is neither engrossed in the selfish pursuit of wordly ambitions and possessions, nor unduly burdened by the trials and sorrows of this present life.

remembering that it is if we suffer with Christ that we shall also be glorified with Him (Rom. viii. 17). The Christian's eyes are often on the horizon as he waits expectantly for the coming of his Lord, who will one day return to usher in His eternal kingdom of righteousness and peace.